Julian Rush—Facing the Music

Julian Rush—Facing the Music

A Gay Methodist Minister's Story

As told to Lee Hart Merrick

Writers Club Press
San Jose New York Lincoln Shanghai

Julian Rush—Facing the Music
A Gay Methodist Minister's Story

Writers Club Press
an imprint of iUniverse.com, Inc.

For information address:
iUniverse.com, Inc.
5220 S 16th, Ste. 200
Lincoln, NE 68512
www.iuniverse.com

Phil Nash has generously given permission to use an extended quotation from his article about Julian Rush in the October 29, 1981 issue of *Westword*

ISBN: 0-595-19658-6

Printed in the United States of America

In loving memory of David Woodyard, who wrestled both with AIDS and the angels.

I never asked to be the way I am,
And I can't recall a time, just can't remember
When I wasn't the way I am...
Attracted to the wrong sex, brother!
What a disgrace to your poor father and your mother.
I tried to be a friend in need for all the neighborhood,
And labored so intensely to do everything I should.
I knew that dad would like to see me playing ball, or track,
I wanted to be everything I wasn't. Take it back, God.
It's no treat being different, but if that's what I'm to be,
Then please God, let me find a place where I can just be me...
A quiet place, a loving place, my special place.

I tried to do those special things to make my parents proud—
Good grades and popularity; the jock; above the crowd!
But all the while, uneasy. Dating girls, but on the run,
And wishing I was everything I wasn't. It's no fun, God.
I don't like being different, but if that's what I'm to be,
Then please God, let me find a place where I can just be me...
A quiet place, a loving place, my special place.

From the musical play *The Man Who Can Save the Day* by Julian Rush

Introduction

Julian didn't want to do this book. A look of fear crossed his face when I suggested the possibility. Afraid that I had lost the opportunity, I urged him to please take all the time he wanted to consider his answer. I waited a month. Finally, one day late in 1984 the "yes" came, and we began six months of weekly interviews. He faithfully attended these, despite a ridiculous schedule, and even while nearly changing his mind at least three times.

His initial fear was the possibility of causing more pain for his family and friends. They had been through enough. There was also the fear of exposing his weakness and vulnerability, not a style of life common to gentlemen raised in fine Southern tradition. Finally, because he does not feel there is anything particularly dramatic about who he is and what he is (an opinion with which I am at strong odds), he was embarrassed at being singled out from all the lesbian and gay people who also have powerful stories to tell.

Even though I had been acquainted with Julian for fifteen years at the time, and we had developed a mutual trust, this presented some distinct challenges for me. I would need to be careful and gentle in handling subjects which could wound or embarrass. I would be responsible for creating an interview atmosphere that would encourage the honest expression of weakness, vulnerability, pain, depression, anger and fear.

I knew Julian's style was not to draw attention to himself by reviewing his woes. He would tend to emphasize the positive elements, stressing growth, learning, community support and hope. By nature he would hesitate to mention the price of the journey, and even when pressed, would markedly underplay the personal cost. I would have to dig and prod and lead and he would need to maintain confidence that we were doing this together. While I would extract the information and construct the text, we agreed Julian's final approval was essential.

Throughout his story, selected lyrics appear from the musical plays Julian wrote for production in churches where he ministered. While the lyrics speak profoundly to the events with which they are paired here, none were created with direct reference to those events, and many were written years before. However, since songs of musical theater often express the most powerful emotions of the characters, they also manifest the sensitivities of the playwright. In this book, the lyrics reveal emotions emerging during the forty-five years before Julian was able to be honest about the reality that he is a gay person.

As our interviews progressed, and Julian's commitment to the telling of his story became clear despite his ambivalence, I asked what had motivated him to continue. Referring to the musical plays he had written and produced over the years, Julian noted that they were developed as a means of communication. Basing his opinion on all the grateful letters, phone calls and personal contacts which came to him because of the media coverage of his story, Julian was convinced that communicating his experience helps people.

He explained, "There are persons out there who are still living with the assumption that being gay or lesbian is unacceptable, pathetic, unworthy, or just plain despicable. I desperately want those persons to know that life truly does not have to be that way. Of these people, there are many closeted lesbians and gays within the church who need the self-confidence that is provided by having one more person stand up and be counted, by trying to change the system for those to follow. I want the system to be different in the years to come; I want my children to live in a world that is more accepting and affirming than the world in which I grew up. I so hope they will be able to see the exposure of my life, and a bit of theirs, in this book as one of my efforts to leave the world just a little better than when I came in.

"I know that the thinking of people can change. There are many heterosexual people within the church tradition who currently feel homosexuality is too economically threatening for the church to grapple with, or too personally threatening to accept. Yet when I was conducting workshops on human sexuality, I found some of these people chose to change and were able to enlarge their visions. Consciousness-raising actually does work and people do grow and incorporate new ideas, which may be good news for those who have given up on the church. They might even think again about becoming involved in a congregation if they were assured that some positive change is taking place. They need to know that the church isn't just those people who are down on lesbians and gays, but is also composed of people who deeply care and are selflessly committed to the cause of human justice.

"Most of all, my story may give hope and confidence to those gay persons who suffer crushing despair. These are my spiritual brothers and sisters, and I want to be present for them if I can. Telling my story to them and for them is a ministry."

The word minister is from the Latin word for servant—one who serves others. Julian and I seek to serve others through the pages that follow. Many people have helped us generously in this project. We are indebted to them all, honored by their support, and grateful for their active love.

Chapter One

Program Notes
The Man Who Can Save the Day
A Musical Drama by Julian Rush

The youth of Mountain View and First United Methodist Churches in Boulder, Colorado, are pleased to present *The Man Who Can Save the Day*, a musical drama written and directed by Julian Rush, Minister of Education at First Methodist.

The presentation of this play involves young people in a celebration of the earthly ministry of Jesus Christ in a not too distant future. It is a musical love story about today and always…written to show the excitement and freshness of the Christian message as it applies to *all* people and to *all* times. As they work together, our young actors are involved in the same process of struggle and discovery that challenged the first disciples: in dedication to the work of Christ, each imperfect disciple (or actor) finds a place, a task, and an affirmation of self-worth; this is also a major message of the play.

The Man Who Can Save the Day will be performed by 42 junior and senior high school students during their annual Spring Break play tour. The 1981 tour includes performances in nine cities: Amarillo, Ft. Worth, and Richardson, TX; Oklahoma City, OK; Dodge City, KS:

and Boulder, Denver, Longmont and Pueblo, CO. Since his appointment to Boulder's First Methodist Church in 1976, the Reverend Rush has presented on tour his original musical plays *P.T. Was Here, JesusSong,* and *The Rise and Fall of the Girl.*

* * *

I was born gay, I'm quite sure of that.

I was born in Mississippi, the grandson of a horse-loving urologist and one of two children of a pharmacist. My mother and dad spent most of their days, except Sunday, working at the drugstore. During my preschool and elementary years, because I was so sheltered, I was the stock definition of a sissy. I had very low self-esteem and desperately wanted to be popular, but didn't know how. I had no involvement in athletics because I was afraid of physical combat, and I was insecure because I didn't know how to play sports like the other boys my age. By the time I was five, my grandparents had bought a Shetland pony for me, and one day prepared to take pictures of me on the pony. I remember my mother coming into the bedroom and finding me donning all sorts of hats, trying to costume myself for the occasion, and being told rather curtly that little boys didn't do that.

When the time came to climb into the saddle, I was put into place, and the pony started bucking. The pony was subsequently sent to be trained. Later, when once more I was placed on the pony, he bucked again. Both experiences frightened me, and while I never rode horses after that, I did enjoy riding in the buggy with my granddad. In later years, I would go with him on his midweek afternoon off and on Saturday to spend time with him while he worked with his horses.

During the summer, all the kids in the neighborhood would play outside after it got dark, usually choosing games like hide and seek. One evening we were all sitting on the sidewalk under the street lamp, talking in the warm Mississippi twilight. This was about the same time I had refused to ride horses anymore, and one of the boys, Richard Fuller, started teasing me about being a sissy. I can still remember that long attack on me and his saying, with a sneer, how he could visualize me in my little curls. I stared at the sidewalk the whole time, hating him for what he was doing, but not having the ego strength to talk back or to run away

> *Antwerp Ant:*
> Being down is like down on the ground
> With nobody, no place to go;
> When the big creatures push you around,
> And they make you feel…Oh, I don't know.
> It's a feeling that's more like a pain in your heart,
> And you feel like…you feel like…a worm.

> From *The Resurrection Thing* by Julian Rush

When I was six and in the first grade, some of the older kids were slamming the restroom door and locking the younger kids inside. I was so terrified by this that I once ran all the way home at recess to go to the bathroom, because I was afraid to go into the restroom at school.

In later elementary school, I remember being hurt by my dad in a way that he never realized. I enjoyed artistic activities such as drawing, painting, clay modeling and weaving. On this occasion, I was knitting a yarn bag for my dad's golf balls, just prior to a visit from relatives. My dad's older sister and her husband had four boys, all involved in athletics, and the oldest son was about my age. Because they would be arriving soon, dad asked me to put away the bag I was working on for him, explaining that Uncle Carroll's kids didn't do that sort of thing, and they might not understand. I'm sure my dad didn't intend to be cruel, but I was devastated.

Parents of Marion Park Elementary School boys anticipated that all male children in fifth and sixth grades would go out for football, and I became involved because I didn't have any choice. During practices at school, I can remember going through motions without understanding what we were doing or why. All I knew was that I didn't like it and I didn't want to be there. The coaches would draw plays on the blackboard, but I could never remember which one was which and was never sure where I was supposed to go. I'm sure my poor retention was the result of not wanting to be involved.

Our team's major debut was the night we were scheduled to play a team from another elementary school during the half time of a high school football game. When I donned my uniform that night, I was taken next door to be shown off to a friend and neighbor who was a former high school coach. I remember wondering how I could escape the predicament I was in. All during our game that night, I sat on the bench hoping my number wouldn't be called. When the coach asked if there was anyone who had not played, I remained quiet, so I never had to face the test. Somehow, I ultimately escaped playing football altogether. Yet there were still many embarrassing moments at school and at other places when I made up lame excuses to avoid playing football, softball, or whatever.

I was not very successful with swimming either. When I was in elementary and junior high school, my parents were members of the country club. Despite swimming lessons, I was still trying to swim with my head above water because when my nose went underwater I always got strangled. As a result, it was the end of the second summer before I ever learned to swim successfully. All my friends, the same age as myself, were swimming in the deep part of the pool, while I had to stay in the shallow end. It was the same story at Scout camp; for two summers I had to stay in the beginners' pool while all my friends went on to the advanced classes. It was humiliating for me and I could tell it was embarrassing for my folks.

By the time I reached sixth grade, I had been teased so much about being a sissy that I began trying very hard to act macho, or at least non-sissy. About that same time, I had a crush on another boy in my room. I wouldn't have known at that time how to even talk about what I felt, but I look back now and know that what I felt was actually romantic love. At age eleven, I had a crush on a boy. While studying geography, the chapter that gave fire to my imagination concerned the Amazon River basin and its people. For years after, I fantasized about living there with one or another classmate from my school, always male, but not always the same person. The fantasies were not always sexual, but they always involved an intense love relationship. The imagined object of my affection was my significant other, and we lived, in love together, deep in the Amazon basin.

In my hometown, people designated as gay were viewed as poor, wretched people to be pitied, and were spoken of in hushed tones. I recall my grandmother taking me on a bus trip to Miami, Florida to visit her relatives. Boarding the bus with us were two young adult males, demonstrably effeminate. As my mother said goodbye to us, she cautioned us to find seats in a different section of the bus, away from "those two boys." With this kind of upbringing, it's no wonder that my adolescent mind wanted to suppress anything which might suggest that I had a gay orientation. I could not allow myself to even consider that I might be "that way."

King:
Now an ant is an ant
And a worm is a worm
But an ant has to crawl
And a worm has to squirm,
So an ant shouldn't bother
Befriending a worm
Since a worm cannot crawl
And an ant cannot squirm
We're different and different we'll stay,
It's just God's will.
It's just God's way.

From *The Resurrection Thing* by Julian Rush

Freak show! Come and see the freak show!
It's the finest little piece of entertainment
That you will likely find anywhere
truly rare
beyond compare
So come and take a little peek at the freak show!
Come and see the freak show!
Sssh! This is probably the most controversial of all—our
token gay, Quixote!
This one doesn't dress in pink. Doesn't swish.
Doesn't even wish that he were different.
Tsk! Tsk! Tsk!
No flair. Just a very simple model. Every group should
have one.

From *The Man Who Can Save The Day* by Julian Rush

Of course, avoidance of undesirables in the Southern culture was not
limited to people presumed to be homosexual. Our world was also perme-
ated by the viewpoint that whites were superior to blacks, and since blacks
were inferior, they were not to be considered as friends or associates. I can
remember early on asking why the black people employed in our household always had to eat in the kitchen. The black man who did our yard
work was always given water in a jar rather than a glass, as if he had some
kind of black germs which might contaminate our household. The maid
was told that when she used the bathroom, she was to raise the toilet seat
and sit on the porcelain rim.

By junior high school, I knew there was something about that social
structure which didn't make sense to me. Just as relationships with effeminate people did not trouble me, neither did associating with black folks. I
became a part of several integrated church meetings during my high
school years—meetings that never felt difficult or unnatural.

I'm not aware of anything in my life at this time that would have nurtured my discomfort with the Southern viewpoint. Rather, it was almost as if my genes were different from the majority of those in my culture, causing me to perceive the world differently. Here I was, birthed into a culture that saw realities in a way that I found foreign. Looking back, I wonder if this realization was a part of the whole process of somehow understanding myself as a minority and comprehending that the world wasn't, in fact, the way it was being presented to me.

My parents had little social life outside of the contacts made through their work at the drugstore. At the time, I felt they were not social enough, but to come home to a quiet, uncluttered evening after a busy day at the store was probably recreation enough for them. On the other hand, my grandparents, who lived next-door, loved company. There were frequent overnight or weekend visitors and always large gatherings for special holidays such as Thanksgiving, Easter and Christmas. Consequently, I grew up in one house where the life style was quiet and private, and right next door was a household that was always a hub of activity. My grandparents made numerous trips and visits, and often I was included. While my parents were not well off economically, my grandparents were financially comfortable, and they saw to it that I had clothes, trips, and money for social activities. I never wanted for anything, and grew up in a very stable family environment with the best of possible worlds. But creaturely comforts could not prevent the junior high school years from being a nightmare for me.

Since I had always been sheltered, attending the only junior high school in a city of forty thousand people was frightening. I was still afraid of any kind of conflict and still ashamed of being unable to participate effectively in sports. The shame was not the competitive nature of the game as much as my inexperience. I had never played baseball or football, and I didn't want to be embarrassed by having people discover that I didn't know how to catch or throw a ball (basic things that *any* boy ought to know). In my early junior high years, my parents insisted that I take golf lessons at the country club, but the game didn't interest me. As a result, I only played golf once and never picked up the clubs again. I was also becoming involved in extracurricular school activities so that my time schedule provided an easy out.

In seventh grade, I joined the band to avoid the Physical Education requirement. Later on, in high school, that decision proved to be a constructive move, because I became student conductor and drum major, both positions of esteem in that particular high school. I also became active on the newspaper staff and in art-related activities. I managed to become so busy that I didn't even take my studies very seriously. Several of my friends attended the junior high group at the downtown Methodist Church, so I became active there, and, in addition, became a Boy Scout and a part-time employee in my parents' drugstore. With this kind of involvement, any possible terrors were offset by a swirl of happy times. I desperately wanted to be popular and accepted, but didn't know how to go about making that happen.

During this junior and senior high period, I had a creeping realization that my gayness was a dangerous skeleton in the closet that had to be sealed off forever. I could not allow this specter to exist at my conscious level, because I would not be able to handle it. Early in seventh grade, I had sent off for a Charles Atlas exercise course. I constructed my own dumbbells of bricks and Lincoln logs and began to build up my body. I also started trying to be consciously masculine in the way I talked and moved.

I realized that I thought differently about males than did my male peers. My Boy Scout troop was the largest in town, fifty or sixty members, and we had frequent weekend retreats. There was always a lot of sexual banter. As far as I knew, this was just the fun and games of adolescent expression for most of the boys. For me, the sexual overtones became the focus of a very private celebration of my own. I could fantasize all sorts of sexual scenes with other boys and tuck them away in the privacy of my own memory bank. This was a time when my sexual awareness began to heighten, and I began to understand that in building up my body, the pictures of the bodybuilders in the instruction magazines were more arousing than just interesting. At the same time, I knew that the genteel Southern society in which I lived labeled such feelings as a big "**NO**."

> *Chancellor and various others:*
> Bend toward the middle and don't disagree.
> It's all for the good of the group.
> Don't try to live individually.
> It's all for the good of the group.
> We're one happy family who sticks together,
> So don't venture out all alone in the weather.
> We're brotherly birds
> Of a sisterly feather.
> It's all for the good of the group.
> Learn to be tactful and always discreet.
> It's all for the good of the group.
> Try hard to avoid being too commanding.
> For those who conform, life is never demanding,
> So donate your thoughts to a mass understanding.
> It's all for the good of the group.

From *The Rise and Fall of the Girl* by Julian Rush

In spite of societal pressure and my determination to deny my gayness, my orientation seemed insistent upon making itself known and affirmed. During my early high school years, I happened to meet and become sexually involved with a young adult male who was a little older than I was. In the early days of our being together, we maintained a polite distance. As time went on, however, we both became acutely aware of the strong energy that flowed between us. We would make eye contact and blush. We could feel the excitement of one another's close proximity. Without even being able to acknowledge it at first, we knew that a powerful romantic feeling was there and we both knew that the other felt it as well.

Finally we found ourselves one day alone in a private place together and we literally fell into one another's arms. We felt a deep love for each other and remained romantically linked until he had to move elsewhere. The fear of discovery and the feeling on both our parts that our love could never be realized made the parting easier, and gradually we turned one another loose. During the summer preceding my junior year in high school, I decided to bury all of my secret yearnings, try to forget that they ever existed, and face the new school year as person reborn. That summer a religious experience also helped me as I tried to reinvent myself.

During high school, the church became a very important focus in my life. I regularly attended the downtown Methodist church youth group, and my friends there deemed it reasonable to elect me President of the Youth Fellowship. The minister informed me in a very kind way that my leadership was wanted but not appropriate unless I became a member of that church. Since many of my Rush relatives were Methodists, switching churches posed no difficulty for me or for my family. Shortly thereafter, I officially became a Methodist and MYF President.

My grandmother was a loyal Methodist and devoted Christian. Every summer, I joined her family tradition of many years by spending two weeks with her at a camp meeting in south Mississippi. There was an open tabernacle with sawdust floor and wooden pews built especially for the annual camp meeting. Around the tabernacle was grouped a semicircle of cabins, populated by families which had been attending the camp meetings for many generations. The summer between my tenth and eleventh grade years, I had something akin to a conversion experience at the camp meeting. I have no recollection of what the minister said on that particular night, or exactly what happened. I only know that I lay awake that night seriously thinking about my own destiny for the first time.

(In the following excerpt, Vincent is the Christ-figure:)

One morning I heard Vincent speak, as by his chair I
knelt,
And for some reason, I began to tell him how I felt.
So Vincent took my hands in his and looked in my face.
He called me brother. Come with me, he said.
We have a place for you.
A quiet place at last.
A loving place at last.
My special place at last.

From *The Man Who Can Save the Day* by Julian Rush

That experience impacted me so much that my life was actually
changed. At school that fall, for the first time I became a conscious
Christian. I began to care about other people in a selfless way I had not
known before. I found myself beginning to gain popularity, something I
had desperately wanted all my life. But with it came a negative effect that
stayed with me for many years. I began to satisfy my acceptance needs
with popularity rather than with performance. Good grades, responsible
follow-through in assignments, and a mature prioritizing of my activities
and plans began to be less important than popularity.

There was a boy a year ahead of me in school who was very well liked.
Tony Sansone became my model/hero. I watched him, scrutinizing everything he did, patterning my actions after his. My popularity increased
markedly, and by twelfth grade I was designated class "favorite." I was chosen one of three male "brother" sponsors of the high school sorority. In my
two years of junior college, I was class favorite for two years and was chosen Mr. MJC (Meridian Junior College) an unprecedented two years in a
row. I was selected Pledge Trainer of my fraternity at Millsaps College the
following year, and President the next.

With all of this attention, I fell into the habit of living my life in order
to please others. I strove so hard to be everything other people wanted me

to be that I began to lose sight of who I was and who I wanted and needed to be. Of course, I did all the acceptable and appropriate things socially— dating girls, attending parties, and behaving in general as the good hetero- sexual I wasn't. As I look back now, I realize that in high school many of the girls I dated were good buddies. The relationships were platonic. In my eyes and in the eyes of my family, I was just having a great time in high school. When I was chosen as one of the male sponsors of the sorority, it was not only an honor socially, but a lot of fun, since so many of the girls in the group were my good buddies and "sisters", so to speak. I was prob- ably a much more fitting mascot than either they or I realized.

During all this time, any awareness I might have had regarding my sex- ual orientation was so disturbing that I immediately suppressed it. The more I suppressed, the more skillful I became at denial. To the detriment of my studies, I always kept myself involved in a flurry of activities. I was crowding my life so that I didn't have time to stop and think about any- thing, and because my junior college classes were in the same building with the high school, I took full advantage of an extended, overly-pro- grammed high school experience, leaving no time for change or reflection.

Soon after joining the Methodist church, I began to participate in Methodist youth work on a statewide level. I held three different offices, and in the fourth year became the state Methodist Youth President. In this posi- tion of wide recognition, I found great satisfaction. The other youth with whom I worked became close friends and an invaluable support system.

The Presidential position also became a creative outlet. All kinds of statewide events were held during that four-year period, and I was able to write skits, songs, plays and a plethora of programs.

My eleventh grade year marked the beginning of my full-scale public creativity. In my community, with the junior college housed with the high school, we referred to the two years of junior college as the thirteenth and fourteenth grades. The fourteenth graders had done a musical presenta- tion for the past three years as a money-raiser. As an eleventh grader, I became involved in their final event—a variety show constructed around the twelve calendar months and entitled *Happy Holidays*. I helped with the staging and music for four of the twelve months depicted. The fourteenth graders recognized me for my talent at the dinner following the performance by presenting me with a special certificate. This was a unique honor for me, since I was one of only three eleventh graders involved.

In twelfth grade, with permission from the principal, I wrote my first full-length musical comedy for our senior class as a money-raising project. Entitled *Beaux and Belles*, it featured three of my original songs, along with the rest of the score borrowed from elsewhere. It was the story of Shriners and showgirls who took a trip from New York to Miami for a Shrine convention. What had started as a positive experience with the fourteenth grade variety show became a creative zenith for me. After *Beaux and Belles*, the tradition was set. The school administration and my class came to expect one of my musicals as the fund-raising vehicle for our class each year.

In my first year of junior college, I wrote a musical called *Convivialo*, and both the play and the musical score were all mine. *Convivialo* was the story of a wandering minstrel, Robert the Rover, in the Robin Hood/knights era. Robert, a Shane-like character, wanders into Convivialo Castle, untangles all the interpersonal messes and walks off into the sunset. The success of the musical that year was overwhelming. The following year, I wrote a musical play set in an English countryside titled *Revelers Road*. This was a more ambitious production, with dream sequences and a smoke machine. Since the plot was more developed and the music more intricate, I considered it a step forward in my creative development.

Part of the driving force behind my burst of creativity was, I am sure, a mechanism to escape thinking about or dealing with my orientation. The works I had created were always safely and respectably heterosexual. Only years later, while I served at First United Methodist Church in Boulder, Colorado, did I finally put a gay character on the stage. By then, the energy of my real self was becoming difficult to restrain. My public creativity became altered in Boulder because awareness of my sexual orientation was beginning to burst into my consciousness like grass springing through cracks in pavement. But that was long after the two years at Meridian Junior College and graduation from Millsaps College, which lead to five years of theological school and then ministry.

During seminary, the thesis for my Master of Sacred Theology was a three-act musical titled *On Friday with the Bluejays*. After seminary, I became youth minister at First United Methodist Church in Fort Worth, Texas, and in my first year, the youth president wanted to put together a variety show to raise money. I suggested that we add a story line to help hold it together. The production was quite successful and started a pattern in my youth work—using musical drama as a vehicle for ministry.

While obtaining a master's degree in drama at the University of Denver School of Drama in 1969, *Jesus Christ Superstar*, the Oratorio, was just becoming popular. I was taking a directing course from a very innovative member of the faculty, who agreed to allow me to stage the Oratorio for my final assignment. I combined forces with a dynamic choral director at Park Hill United Methodist Church in Denver, and we staged *Superstar* with actors and actresses from the DU Theater Department, and the youth choir and rock band from the church.

When my directing class from school came to view an early rehearsal, there were numerous suggestions and some doubts as to whether I could make the play a success. My classmates were unaware of my past experience with musical productions, and did not know, as I did, that I really knew how to do this and do it well. Performance night we set up one hundred and fifty chairs, since I understood that a good deal of interest had been created in the production, but I was not prepared for what took place. More than seven hundred people arrived. The room was packed, the energy level was high, and the presentation was a resounding success. I received accolades from audience members, class members and the instructor, which allowed me to leave DU in a blaze of glory.

Chapter Two

With the completion of the Master's Degree in Drama, my life stage was set for a lively career in youth ministry, sharing the biblical message not only in traditional ways, but also in theatre and song. The Program notes of *The Man Who Can Save the Day*, below, illuminate the professional journey that brought me to Colorado and to the unexpected events that were to follow.

> About the author of *The Man Who Can Save The Day*:
>
> Julian Rush is a graduate of Millsaps College, in his native Mississippi. He received his Master of Divinity and Master of Sacred Theology degrees from Perkins School of Theology at Southern Methodist University. Julian's first position as minister of youth was at First Methodist Church in Fort Worth, Texas. From there he moved to Denver to continue his education. He staged *Jesus Christ Superstar* while attending Denver University and received his MA in drama in 1971. Since then, drama has been an important part of his youth ministry in Colorado Springs and Boulder churches.

During my first year in Colorado Springs, I wrote a one-act musical play entitled *Quest*, a story of the birth, crucifixion and resurrection of Jesus. When the youth of First Methodist Church presented it just prior to Christmas, the play was successful enough that we began to consider taking it on tour during spring break in March. Within a few weeks, the younger brother of the lead boy in the play came to me seeking a part. Since I had not met him before, I asked him to do some reading for me and discovered he was a natural comedian. Thus, when *Quest* went on tour that spring, there was a new part written into the play for Jeff. The story took on a fresh dimension because of the added humor and several tailor-made songs, sung by the new character. The experience with *Quest* made me appreciate the value of using all materials at hand. Frequently I held up writing the final draft of a play until I was sure who was available and what they were able to do. The result was that many of the plays were custom-written for the lead performers. There were times, of course, when the material added was more extraneous, especially for the minor parts, but frequently the original script benefited greatly from the embellishments, adaptations and changes.

What started out as a particular attempt to involve one young man turned into a successful stylistic and ministerial approach. Jeff was unique and delightful in his own way, but prior to the plays he hadn't found any way to plug into the church system. I was challenged to try reaching him, so I arranged for us to do a number of musical productions together. I wrote *P. T. Was Here*, a musical drama based on the life of Paul of Tarsus, as a vehicle for Jeff because he was such a natural on the stage. The style of the play is patterned after P.T. Barnum—Paul's missionary journeys being conceived as a traveling minstrel show. It was fun creating material for him, and the involvement gave him a place in the church.

The experiences with *Quest* and *P.T.* undoubtedly sharpened my sense of calling in terms of using musical comedy to communicate the faith. Some few kids might read the story of Paul with total empathy, but most probably experienced a sincere lack of interest. To put Paul's life on stage in a situation with contemporary elements and spirited music brought the reality of his struggle alive. One young man came to me after the first production of *P.T. Was Here* and confided that because of his involvement with the play, he had gained an understanding of the Christian faith he had never experienced before. He felt that his life was changed.

The depth of the spiritual atmosphere created by the group involvement in the plays was well-illustrated one evening when we were touring *Quest*. A boy came to me before the performance one evening and confided that he thought he was gay. He asked that he be allowed to tell the whole cast after the performance that night what he was feeling and have them pray for him. Fortunately, the group was sleeping overnight in the church, so after the audience had left and we were alone, we gathered the youth together for the young man to tell his story. I encouraged all forty-five youth and counselors to surround him. Everyone stood very close together with arms entwined, and anyone who wanted could speak or pray. The experience probably lasted no more than fifteen or twenty minutes, but it was very highly charged. The possibility of this time together grew directly out of the openness the play had fostered.

> *Troupe:*
> We got the good news, the good news, it's true,
> We got the good news, the good news for you.
> The tales that you've heard about Jesus are true.
> And that's gotta be good news for you!
>
> We got some good news that we want to share
> With all the Gentiles and Jews everywhere.
> The tales that you've heard about Jesus are true,
> And that's gotta be good news,
> And that's gotta be good news,
> And that's gotta be good news for you. Hey!
>
> From *P.T. Was Here* by Julian Rush

In the middle seventies, many youth were in a turbulent state. Our youth group was no exception. As we toured a musical play one spring, our bus was making a loop through El Paso, Texas, and Carlsbad, New Mexico. Our first stop in El Paso was a suburban church in a well-to-do neighborhood. The building, surrounded by its own parking lot, occupied one square block. We arrived on a Saturday night, and while the kids were unpacking the bus, the chaperones and I decided to drive one of the vans to a convenience store two blocks away to buy snacks for the group. As we returned to the church parking lot, the lights of the van caught several naked bodies ducking behind bushes. It took me a minute to realize what was happening. This was the era when all across the country people were "streaking"—running naked through private and public gatherings of all types, and then disappearing. Now our kids, too, were streaking, right there in the middle of suburban El Paso on a Saturday night in the yard of the neighborhood church where we were guests.

I immediately gathered the group together, trying to maintain my composure. Of course, most of those who were involved in streaking were the leads in the play. If they were sent home, the entire production would collapse. As I processed with the group what had happened, we came to the conclusion that the entire tour shouldn't suffer because of the poor judgment of a few. I described the event to the group as stupid, immature and disappointing, but no further action was taken. Later there were parents who denounced my leniency, but I stood by that decision and I still do.

I confess both sympathy and empathy with the playful and spontaneous acts that can occur when two or more young people get together. During my junior and high years, I tried a lot of things myself. One took place just after I received my driver's license. A carload of my friends and I stopped at a neighborhood grocery and stripped several strings of Christmas lights off the large evergreen tree in front of the store. Unscrewing all the lights from the sockets, we traveled across town to the home of a junior high teacher we all knew and disliked. Exhibiting behavior inexplicable to an adult mind, we jumped out of the car, threw the light bulbs at her house yelling, "Hey, blubber bait!," dove back into the car and sped away. *(What were we thinking?!)* I circled the block and stopped before driving back out into the main thoroughfare. One of my friends in the car spied the teacher's husband running toward us at a rather fast clip. I stomped on the accelerator, not even looking to see if traffic was coming. Luckily, we escaped safely, but the license plate number was recorded and by the next day my parents were informed. My safe escape was short-lived—I was grounded, unable to use the car for two months, and was forced to apologize to the teacher in person. Looking back now, I know that the experience must have been very painful for the teacher, yet for us boys at the time, it was just a prank.

As a participant in a more creative prank in high school, I have remained undiscovered until now. In our new library addition, there was a large clear plastic world globe on a wooden stand. We came up with the wonderful idea of putting water and goldfish inside the globe. I borrowed a key from a fellow student who was not supposed to have keys (of course!) and, during a Friday night school dance, two of my friends and I sneaked into the library. We filled the bottom half of the globe with water and added the goldfish. Locking the door, we returned to the dance and told no one. However, there was one problem that we had not anticipated: the weight of the water broke the plastic globe, and the librarian came in the next morning to discover a wet floor and dead fish. There were no damages to floor, furniture or books. The globe was replaced, and the playful cherubs who caused the watery mess were never discovered.

With those types of events in my own background, I admit to having a warm spot in my heart for the streakers and all the other kids responsible for stupid things that were done for fun. In youth ministry I never tolerated intentional destructiveness or blatant unkindness, but for innocuous pranks that were done just for fun, I was never harsh.

On another occasion during my ministry in Colorado Springs, our youth group was returning from a play performance in Pueblo, Colorado. Three of the senior boys who prided themselves on being hell-raisers, and who were also lead characters in the plays, were sitting in the back seat of our old school bus as we returned to our church building through downtown Colorado Springs. The three boys got friends to shield them from observation by the other bus passengers, and with backsides to the window, dropped their trousers and "mooned" downtown Colorado Springs as we traveled through town. As bad luck would have it, a couple on their way to church was driving behind the bus and saw it all. I didn't find out about the escapade until the next day. I had been sitting in the front of the bus with most of the chaperones, and because so many of the youth were standing or moving about the bus aisle, the event was not obvious to the majority of the passengers. I was later chastised and asked, "Why can't you control these kids?" In an undoubtedly unsatisfying response, I replied that I could never second-guess what this group might do next!

Despite these kinds of pranks, one of the things that has always irritated me in the church is the notion of training kids to be the church leaders of tomorrow when many of them are quite capable of being church leaders today. During my ministry, we looked for opportunities to help kids use their leadership skills. The Colorado Springs church did not condone young people smoking, of course, but at one youth event a young man from our group was caught hiding behind one of the buildings smoking. The adult sponsors at the retreat gathered to discuss the situation, and some were prepared to send the offender home. I balked. I gathered the entire group together, adults and youth, and had the boy involved come up to the front of the room. I told all the youth what had happened. Then I read out loud the Biblical story of the woman taken in adultery where Jesus says, "He that is without sin among you, let him first cast a stone at her." (John 8:7) When I finished, I asked the group if they wanted the boy to go home. Not only did they say "no", but it was a resounding "NO!" Some of them even came up and embraced the boy. Had the adults run the show and sent the boy home, they would have undermined the very relationships the conference was designed to develop. I believe that seeking the decision-making resources of the youth group was much more significant for credible ministry. The boy caught smoking did not receive approval for his behavior from anyone, but the whole group learned something specific and genuine about Christian acceptance. I don't recall whether the experience persuaded the young man to stop smoking, but I'm sure he learned a lot about why hiding what you're doing may not be best for you, and what true acceptance does for one's own self image.

I always believed in trusting the group to make its own decisions, and, when possible, letting the kids themselves process problems. In my experience, they always took the responsibility very seriously. While some parents objected to having "kids like that" in a church group (youth who smoke, cuss, drink, or other "naughty" things like that), I find such blackballing to be one of the real sadnesses in the church. We're not called to minister only to those we perceive to be respectable, and in terms of youth, easy to control. We're called to minister to everyone we can, even if, God forbid, it isn't easy.

John:
If the love of this man is gonna live
Then it's through you and me;
If the love that he brought is to be shared,
Our sharing is the key:
And if this great love is gonna last,
Then the hands that do the work in the world,
And the feet that do the walking around, And the lips that
do the speaking to those
That are hungry for life and for love in the world,
They must be, could be, should be, gotta be …
mine, so make love live again.

From *Quest* by Julian Rush

During my last year in Colorado Springs, I received a call from a minister in Dallas about an open position in his church. I flew down for an interview and felt enthusiastic. While the church had a theologically conservative element, the members were very straightforward about wanting me there because I would bring a different perspective.

In the past, Dallas had been Mecca for me, a place where I had attended seminary and experienced incredibly challenging and happy years. While I was pastor for the five years in Fort Worth, making trips to Dallas, only thirty miles away, was always fun. I suppose I looked forward to more of the same.

But after the second interview, I had reservations. I had been seeking a move away from the exclusivity of youth work into a ministry of wider education. On this visit, I was informed that I would be expected to do youth ministry first, and if things went well, "as we know they will," then the job description could be expanded. That arrangement was unsatisfactory to me, causing the central appeal of the job to disappear.

When the opportunity arose to become Education Minister at First United Methodist Church in Boulder, I jumped at the chance. By now I had been married several years and we had two sons. After arriving in Boulder, my wife began work on a graduate program which entailed two summers of study in California. During those two summer terms, I began to realize how much more relaxed I was alone, or alone with the boys. The marriage situation had become very strained, and I chose to work with a therapist for several sessions, trying to decide what I needed to do. When I finally moved out, I contacted friends at First Methodist who had space to rent, and moved my belongings into the furnished downstairs apartment of their home. I was concerned that the boys' home environment not be disrupted more than it had to be, so finding a furnished apartment was ideal. That way the house furnishings could remain intact.

After moving into the apartment, I found myself genuinely alone for the first time in my life. I had never allowed myself to be alone before. I feared I would be terrified, but to my surprise, I wasn't. The physical surroundings couldn't have been better. The home was north of downtown Boulder, perched on a bluff. The apartment opened onto a small patio, and all of downtown Boulder lay below, with the mountains to the southwest. The rooms were warm and inviting, and the wood-paneled living-dining area had a piano and fireplace as well as a large window overlooking the city. One of the two bedrooms had a single bed and the other had two twin beds. Since the boys were with me on weekends most of the time, my twelve-year-old son chose the room with the single bed for himself and my younger son opted to stay with me in the other.

The Olsen family upstairs had a son close to the ages of my sons who helped them get to know kids in the neighborhood. The Olsens were good friends and the living arrangements were comfortable. There was certainly some loneliness, but with the solitude came an opportunity to make contact with my adult self and with my gay self.

I was meeting weekly with Anne Schaef, the therapist, and after the move, dealing with my aloneness became part of our pilgrimage together. In my beginning sessions, I hadn't even begun to realize all that was going on with me. I only knew that I had a feeling of sadness and pain all the time, and that I desperately needed relief.

The longer I worked with Anne, the more I began to focus on some of my major problems. (By then I had obtained a divorce.) One of my issues was an inability to deal with anger. Another was my low self-esteem. I felt poorly about myself; I was a bad person. Why? The closer I got to the issue of my sexual orientation, the more terrified I became. Once in awhile, Anne would throw out a suggestion that I might need to take a look at my sexuality, to re-examine where I was. At first, I unconsciously dodged the suggestions, but as time went on, I began to become more aware of myself: "I'm running from something. I'm afraid to touch it. I'm not really dealing with a gut level issue that's bothering me. I have the lid closed so tight that I'm not even in touch with what this is and what it means." I guess I sensed that my world was crumbling long before it actually did.

In the book, *In Search of God in the Sexual Underworld* by Edwin Clark Johnson, there are a few paragraphs that speak exactly to where I was at that point in my life. The issue was denial.

> Denial is a powerful mechanism in the psyche. We are all familiar with it. We all do it. We all think, "It won't happen to me." When we smoke a cigarette, thinking we won't get cancer, or fail to fasten our seat belts in the car, we're in denial. And when we call things by different names in order to avoid facing their reality, we're in denial.
>
> The things we ignore or prefer not to see are still there: that funny noise in the car's steering mechanism, that lump in our body. Our unconsciousness of them only makes them unmanageable. Things we deny and repress into the unconscious still affect our behavior; we are just not conscious of them. They may become the source of blind emotions or uncontrollable compulsions we cannot understand.
>
> Children may not be told about sexual feelings, but they don't become less sexual. Instead they may deny the feelings, feel guilty, and become compulsively sexual without even quite knowing that what they're doing is sexual. Denial does not solve problems.

It's hard for some people to understand how I could have lived for so many years and not have dealt honestly with my sexual orientation. On some level, I knew that I was gay, but I think I translated that awareness into a different constellation so that I wouldn't have to face the reality. Up to that time, I had not dared to allow myself to deal with the implications of what it might mean to be homosexual. I had constructed a reality for myself that carefully omitted any possibility of having to confront the fact that I was, indeed, gay. During the counseling process with Anne, I began, little by little, to open the door that led into that dark, mysterious room I dared not enter before.

It was almost a game, opening and then shutting the door again for fear of something terrible happening. I don't remember how long the ambivalence went on, but I do know that it took a very long time. I began to realize that in forty-four years, I had never allowed myself to know or affirm who I was. I had never allowed myself to acknowledge the unspeakable, unthinkable "*Thing*"—that unnamable, closeted skeleton.

Once I finally began to talk, my feelings began to spew forth like water from a broken dam. Recognition became information, which in turn became perspective. Suddenly, I could remember having same-sex feelings when I was very young. I recalled at age ten having fantasies of living with a classmate in a love relationship in the Amazon Basin. I could remember one particular individual in scouting who was my hero; I had always idolized him, but now I understand that he was, in fact, a romantic object for me. Some of the sexual banter I had experienced on Boy Scout outings had a very different impact upon me than I thought at the time. I began to see myself in a totally new context; events and feelings I had never understood before began to come clear and make sense. I could understand why, for many years of my life, I had felt like a stranger in a strange land.

In looking back, I'm amazed now at how adept I had become at suppressing my feelings so that I would not see them or remember them for what they were. I went through nearly two years of therapy in college and never once touched the big taboo. Now I understand that when I picked up therapy again in seminary, the driving force which sent me for counseling in the first place was not the need to be honest, but the paranoia that I might somehow have to acknowledge the reality of who I was. My denial skills were so adept that I kept myself from being consciously aware of what I was doing.

One day as I sat in Anne Schaef's office reflecting on what I had done, for the first time I understood how I was living a lie. I was finally opening the feared door and holding it open. After four decades, I was coming into contact with my real self at last.

Once I had worked my way through the initial shock, I was filled with an energizing excitement, a liberation in having the door open for the first time. When I arrived home from counseling with Anne that day, I started crying. I wept almost uncontrollably for about three hours. It was the first time I had cried in at least ten years, and undoubtedly the first time I had cried that fully and completely since I was a child. I had come to terms with being gay, and surprisingly, the experience wasn't devastating at all, but rather a releasing, cleansing resurrection. I was like a person who had been expecting to die from a terminal illness, only to discover that no illness existed.

> When somethin's changed or rearranged,
> When a creature has new color or direction,
> That's resurrection!
>
> When something staid (or plain) has been remade,
> When an unsightly creature changes to perfection,
> That's resurrection!
>
> When something old or something ugly has become
> A something new or something beautiful, then from
> This transformation, you can see, without reflection,
> That's resurrection.

From *The Resurrection Thing* by Julian Rush

Chapter Three

While processing my gayness, I decided to volunteer with the Gay and Lesbian Community Center in Denver because I felt I had to do something to express in a tangible way all the information I was processing. Riding the emotional waves in Anne Schaef's office was always a challenge, but we both agreed that I needed a venue to help me expand my new insights about myself. Even though I had known lesbian/gay people over the years, I needed to experience for myself what I perceived at the time to be a foreign country. I was nervous about the unknown and fearful that someone would spot me as the forty-four-year-old neophyte that I was.

For most of my life, I had lived in a world which felt very secure. People knew who I was and what I could do. I didn't have to prove myself to anyone. But here I was, entering a new arena where almost no one knew me. Once I sat down with Carol Lease, the Center coordinator, I found her to be very reassuring. She suggested that I become involved with both peer counseling and phone answering services.

I began driving to Denver on my day off to answer the phone at the Center, which allowed me to meet a lot of people and groups with whom I had never had any contact. I was amazed at the number of people who came to the Center or called there seeking AA groups. Soon I learned how high the alcoholism rate was and continues to be in the lesbian/gay community. Certainly it makes sense that people are likely to acquire a few coping challenges when they are told from birth, subtly or otherwise, that being lesbian/gay is no damned good. I'm sure many who find themselves trapped by drinking initially don't even know why they connected with alcohol. They just know that drinking temporarily relieves some of that ongoing, nameless pain.

The phone work was particularly appealing to me because I was put in frequent contact, with so many different people. I learned very quickly that there was no "typical" anyone in the lesbian/gay community. There were gay women who didn't want to be referred to as lesbians because they felt it had a negative political connotation. There were also lesbians who wouldn't stand to be called anything else.

On the male side, there were screaming queens who wore flagrant clothing and delighted themselves in being effeminately expressive. There were also cowboys, leather guys, and those who looked like anyone else on the street. I discovered that the varieties within the lesbian/gay community were as numerous as those without, yet all of us shared the commonality of same-sex orientation, and, for most, the pain of rejection as well. That commonality provided a bond that I could not have understood previously.

Awareness of that sense of community drove me to a cause I still champion. I want to do all I can to encourage people to accept themselves and others as they are. That doesn't mean we'll ever agree on everything, but we can always explore together the wider boundaries of our uniqueness—boundaries that reach far beyond what we perceive as our differences.

> *Milltown woman:*
> Someday, like tomorrow, like tomorrow, I can see
> Someday, we'll awaken, we'll awaken and be free.
> The future ahead keeps us going
> With promises too dark to see.
> Unknowns lie beyond the horizon,
> But it's our one and only guarantee that
> Someday, like tomorrow, we'll awaken and be free.
> Someday, like tomorrow, like tomorrow I can see
> Someday, we'll awaken, we'll awaken and be free.
> The future's ahead. Let's go meet it.

Remember, the word's persevere.
We'll tell old man trouble to beat it
Because the only way is up from here, and
Someday, like tomorrow, we'll awaken and be free.

From *Don't Take It So Hard, Mr. Johnson* by Julian Rush

My newfound freedom was producing changes in me that I found to be exciting. The unfolding understanding of myself was so empowering that I felt more and more energized about who I was and what I was becoming. I was too enthused to worry about anyone discovering my sexual orientation and what hardship that might cause for me.

The freeing and energizing self-realization process had come surging up in me like a fountain, and the fountain continued to flow. I felt I had to share it beyond my therapist Anne, and beyond the Center. I wanted to share it with other people in my life who mattered to me.

People changing; rearranging;
Possibilities abounding;
Opportunities astounding;
Love to see endlessly.
Life Force! Life Force! Surging!
Life Force! Longing to be free!

From *The Man Who Can Save The Day* by Julian Rush

I don't think there was one specific time when I told my sons The Big Secret. I was always candid with the boys about sexuality. I assisted with human sexuality workshops during my sons' younger years, so they had access to information written specifically for children and youth concerning sexuality. Talking about gayness was a part of the fabric of talking about sexuality in general. My base of operation for workshops was the Sexual

Information and Resource Center in Boulder, which owned a large collection of well-written children's books, and I had read many with both sons. There were questions along the way, but they occurred on a gradual basis.

"Does a gay man feel the same about men as non-gay men feel about women?"

"Why are some gay people really different-looking and acting and others just like everyone else?"

Since they had been raised to believe that all different kinds of human beings are equally acceptable, black or white, male or female, short or tall, gay or straight, there was also the question, "Why do people think it's wrong to be gay?"

As my own awareness about my orientation grew, their awareness grew as well. I never felt I changed as a father; I just continued being who I was. Only the context was different. I could affirm who I was and not apologize. My sons did have to deal with the reactions of their friends to my sexual orientation, but interestingly enough, compared to our divorce, it seemed to be the lesser of two deeply emotional events in their lives. Both sons now agree that the divorce of their parents was more traumatic for them than dealing with my gayness.

The members of First United Methodist Church of Boulder also experienced both of these deeply emotional events—the divorce of their pastor of education and youth, and then later, the discovery of his sexual orientation.

I had developed a close personal relationship with some of the adult youth workers. We were people who had not only worked together, but played together as well. We had been on youth tours together, and had lived and laughed and prayed through a variety of experiences over five years. These people were with me through my separation and divorce, and I trusted them deeply, so it was only natural that I wanted to share my new level of evolution with them.

I called these friends on the phone and asked them to meet together in my office. Despite my enthusiasm, I was very nervous preceding the gathering, so when everyone had arrived, I came immediately to the point, telling them why I brought them together, and explaining what was going on in my life. They were all supportive, just as I expected them to be. Their facial expressions, body language and words all reflected the same acceptance. To my relief, my sexual orientation didn't matter at all, and not one of them seemed surprised.

I should have realized that the play I had written and produced the previous year paved the way for my coming out. Constructed around the theme of a modern day Jesus with disciples, *The Man Who Can Save The Day* carried a specific social and Biblical message. Each of the disciples was a social reject of one kind or another. Among them was a person who stuttered, one who was crippled, a fat man, a militant Chicano activist, an alcoholic woman, and a gay male. One of the adult youth workers in the meeting that day told me the song sung by the gay character (quoted at the opening of this book) had come through so vividly she felt it had to be my own song.

What I had originally expected to be a difficult task turned out to be easy and even enjoyable. I talked with my youth workers about my future plans, and we all agreed that there was no reason to make a stir about my new awareness. I think we all expected to keep the news quiet and go on from there.

The affirmation and support was exhilarating to me, and I felt compelled to share my budding awareness by phone with the man who had originally hired me at Boulder, former senior minister and now Bishop Cal McConnell.

Around that same time, I had a speaking engagement on the campus of the University of Northern Colorado for a graduate class in human sexuality, and my topic was life as a gay minister. In the class was a woman who knew the current senior minister in my church previously. After the class she called him and, knowingly or unknowingly, revealed the news he was yet to hear from me. With my enthusiastic sharing as background, the organizational wheels began to turn.

Group:
Quiet night, clear sky,
But all's not right and I know why
There's trouble in the air
And soon there'll be trouble everywhere.
Chaos coming down
On this old town, Chaos all around.

From *Don't Take It So Hard, Mr. Johnson* by Julian Rush

I was so enthused about what was happening to me, I was naive about what the possible ramifications could be. The senior minister was aware that he was not among the first to know about my news. He had heard it from his predecessor, the minister I had called first, and had also heard it from the graduate student in the human sexuality class. When I finally did sit down with my boss and I told him that I had shared my news with the youth workers, he must have felt slighted that he was among the last to know. Still, he listened with concern and stated that he felt it was his responsibility to inform the Staff-Parish Relations Committee—the church committee similar to a human resources/personnel committee in the business world. With so many people already informed, he judged that the news could spread, and telling the SPR committee would be in both his and my best interest. How untrue that assumption turned out to be for me!

I expected that the senior minister would share my news in an affirming manner and assure the SPR Committee that the information, being confidential, meant that business and life could and would go on as usual. According to one of the individuals who attended the meeting, the issue was presented not as information, but as a problem. It was not presented in a low-key manner, but in a tense and uptight way. Despite this, there were some people on the committee who had no problem with the revelation. Some members were unsure of how they felt, but the rest were adamantly opposed to my staying in the church at all, now that they knew who I really was.

The night of the meeting I was alone in my apartment, working on the sermon I was scheduled to preach on Sunday. The topic was Abraham and Isaac, and the theme was "risking it all." The thrust of the message was that a Christian is called to live a life of faith, to live on the cutting edge of faith, much like Abraham was doing in daring to go far enough in faith to consider sacrificing his son because he thought that was what God wanted him to do.

Early in the evening I was already uneasy about the meeting under way. Realistically, I knew that everyone would not take the news in a positive way. I had first assumed that even those who didn't go for the idea would at least accept the confidential information and tuck it away. As time wore on that night, my hopeful attitude began to fail. One minute I was saying to myself, "The church can't possibly boot me out; I've spent too much effort and I've been here too long for them to toss me away." Then immediately I'd flip to, "Oh yes they can! I could be out on the street tomorrow with no job and nowhere to go. What would I do?"

During the year prior, I had entertained some thoughts of someday going into some other related vocation, but I knew that the timing had to be right. Because of that vocational counseling, it became clear to me that the world of business didn't recognize ministry as viable. I knew that no one "out there" would accept my skills as marketable. I reviewed in my mind the worst possible scenario. I'd spent all this time training to be a minister and working in churches for seventeen years and now it could end. I could not jump easily from ministry into something else, or even into a ministry-related vocation without a lot of groundwork and multiple connections. Now I was about to be phased out of the only vocation—the calling—I knew, with literally no place to go. My better judgment kept telling me that such a scenario wasn't possible, but my worse judgment was taking over.

I had heard horror stories of gay people being exposed in their workplaces. They were called before their superiors, dismissed, and ordered to disappear overnight. I fantasized being called into my senior minister's office in the presence of the SPR Committee the next day and told to clear everything out of my office and leave.

There's a scene in *Guess Who's Coming to Dinner* that had impressed me enough when I saw the movie that I continued to remember it. When Katherine Hepburn's daughter comes home with the black man she plans to marry, Hepburn discovers that her company secretary is a bigot and fires her. I remember Hepburn saying to her, "Take anything in the office that might possibly remind me that you've been here, and get quietly and permanently lost." I knew the same thing could happen to me.

I felt so dispensable that night. It would be easy for the congregational leader to minimize my importance and sweep me under the carpet to avoid controversy. I had no control over my own destiny. I'd never felt such powerlessness in my whole life.

As the evening wore on, I grew increasingly restless. I took my papers from the table and moved to the chair by the fireplace. I moved to the bedroom to work at the desk. I turned on the stereo and the TV to drown out the terrible silence I felt closing in on me. I began walking back and forth in front of the big living room window, stopping from time to time to watch the cars moving below. I sat down at the piano and to play something; I had several books of show tunes and would start at the beginning of a book and work my way through. In the past, playing the piano had always been a release. When angry, frustrated or anxious, I'd sit down and play for a while and work out the emotions. But tonight, the mental scenario wouldn't go away.

I wasn't sure how the church staff members would react. While I had a good relationship all of them, we had never discussed the gay issue and I didn't know how they felt. And the youth; how would they respond? Again, I thought most of them would be supportive, but I didn't know. Or parents; would they be threatened with the idea of a gay minister having access to their kids? I had not told my landlords. Would they ask me to move out?

The idea of having to tell so many people so much all at once was overwhelming. Talking with a few people at a time had been easy. Somehow, until that night, it had not occurred to me that I might have to tell everyone at the same time. Understanding already the sheer energy it took to share something so personal with even one other person, I couldn't imagine how I could muster the strength to face that experience with twenty, thirty, or more. Little did I realize at the time how far-reaching this revelation would become.

Anyone who needed an explanation about what was going on with me in Boulder would have to be told the whole truth; I had not fought through all those months of therapy to continue my long life of lies. I had come to a place where I was freer than I had ever been in my life, and to return to lies at this point was untenable.

The overriding question of that evening came again and again to haunt me. "How could I survive?" I feared I couldn't make a living anywhere but in the church. In my apartment on the edge of a long table was a huge jade tree. Gazing at the tree, I was reminded of the timelessness of dynasties, and how much I was feeling out of sync with time. I was not a part of ongoing life; a crazy "stop the world, I want to get off" had happened to me. The movie of my whole world was suddenly frozen into a single frame, and was being held there.

This was not true of the SPR meeting. Since the senior minister had made a decision that I should not attend the meeting, he had promised to call when the meeting was over, which I expected to be around nine-thirty or ten. Ten o'clock came and went. Ten-thirty. By that time, I was wandering around—going to the kitchen to get a cup of coffee, back to the chair or table or desk, over to the piano, into the bedroom to lie down on the bed and watch TV for awhile. At eleven o'clock, I became frightened. I was like a person with a toothache, with no relief from the pain, who needs to keep moving. The phone finally rang about midnight.

When I answered, I was surprised to find it was not the senior minister but Ed Sandvold, one of my faithful youth workers. Ed, a member of the SPR Committee, was calling to update me on what happened and he spelled out the situation clearly. There were a few people who had supported me in the meeting, but there were definitely more who had not. The outcome looked grim. Ed tried to be reassuring, but he did confess that the senior minister's presentation had not been particularly supportive. There were some at the meeting who felt that a gay minister on the staff at First Church was unthinkable, one of whom wanted me out immediately. There were also those in a more moderate position who weren't quite sure how they felt about the issue itself and the implications for the church. Then there were the few members who were strongly supportive. The rest of the meeting was spent discussing why I should or should not be asked to leave.

Ed didn't talk long because I told him I was waiting for a call from the senior minister, and I was eager to compare Ed's message with what would certainly follow. Within five minutes the phone rang again. It was the boss, and he presented the situation as much less drastic. He was scheduled to leave town for the weekend, but he informed me that plans had changed. The SPR Committee had decided that under the circumstances, I should not preach on Sunday. Rather, he would return early and preach himself. Then we would all convene on Sunday evening to talk about my situation—the Committee, the District Superintendent, and the two of us. Meanwhile, I was to lie low, stay away from the church, and definitely not be around on Sunday morning.

Despite these instructions, he said several times that I shouldn't worry. *Shouldn't worry?* I knew by then there was plenty to worry about. Everything wasn't all right and wouldn't be all right. Now I was I more frightened than ever—it appeared my life in the church was coming to an end.

Group:
The sky is blue…and the sun is bright.

You're a' ridin' high...'cause the world's all right.
But then fizzle thump thump thump
fizzle thump thump thump
drizzle bump bump bump
Ssssssss. (The car grinds to a halt.)
You got trouble. Mm hum!

Hank:
It just can't be!

Group:
Oh yes it can.
You got trouble. Mm hum!

Hank:
But Lord, why me? I drove the best I can!

From *The Trials and Tribulations of Hank Cohen* by Julian Rush

As the SPR meeting concluded, the question of confidentiality was raised. "Do we need to keep this a secret?" The senior minister indicated confidentiality was not required. "Since Julian had already blabbed his news to the youth workers," confidentiality had already been breached. Following the meeting, of course, the news spread like fire through a dry thicket.

Regina:
All over town the lights go out.
The shades are being drawn
As shelter for encroaching night
Before a trembling dawn.
The tensions mount and tempers flare,
And underneath, the fear

That after what we face ahead,
The skies may not be clear.

From *Don't Take It So Hard, Mr. Johnson* by Julian Rush

Thursday night turned into Friday morning. I wanted to call someone, but didn't want to wake anybody, and even if I did, I didn't know what I'd say if they answered. The Bishop, whom I knew would be supportive, was on vacation. I felt isolated and cut off. I needed to test whether I was over-reacting or being realistic. After the phone calls from Ed and the senior minister, I really wanted and needed someone with me.

I decided I had to go to bed and get some sleep. Often late at night I would go to sleep watching TV, so I tried doing that, without success. Finally, I turned off the TV and lights and for hours tried unsuccessfully to sleep. Around dawn, I gave up, got up, and decided for lack of anything else I would try to clean the house. I remember shining up the bathroom, and sweeping and dusting the living room and bedroom. I felt hopeless and sick. What would I do? Where would I go? Finally the reality became so intense that I broke down and started crying uncontrollably. All the pent up anxiety of the last eight hours just poured out. The more I tried to get control of myself, the harder I cried. I began to realize that I just couldn't endure the crisis alone; I decided to call Doug. Doug McKee was a close minister friend serving at the Wesley Foundation on the University of Colorado campus. I hadn't talked to him about my orientation, but he had been a close friend for a long time, and somehow I knew our relationship would be okay. I finally dialed his number.

There was a weekly ministers' breakfast meeting that both of us often attended, and that morning was the day for the scheduled event. Waking up Doug and his wife, I said to him, "Are you going to the breakfast this morning?" He said no, it was too late to go. My next question was, "Well, could you come over here?"

After a pause, he responded, "Yeah, I guess so."

I said, "Well, maybe I should explain what's going on. I'm gay, the SPR met, and they said I couldn't come back into the building." I had blurted it all out in one sentence and I must have sounded desperate. Doug told me he'd come right over.

I continued to weep after I called him, but by the time he arrived, I was pretty well cried out. He walked in, we sat down, and we talked for three or four hours. He was relieved to find I was sufficiently under control and wouldn't do anything rash. I could deal with it.

(Three fantasy animals hold a musical conversation about animalhood:)

Unicorn:
We're branded as uncivilized and totally unstructured.
Quite a mess!
We're pictured as unmannerly and boorish.
Absolutely no finesse.
But at least we don't attempt to hide aggressions under velvet-covered pride!
I wouldn't be a human. No, I couldn't be a human if I tried!

Grooboo:
We're looked upon as greedy just because we like to eat to stay alive.
We're gluttonous because we have survival as a goal for which to strive,
But at least devouring one another isn't our premeditated way.
I wouldn't be a human. No, I couldn't be a human for a day!

Unicorn:
I'm glad to be an animal. At least I know my place.
I spend no time on arrogance, or failure and disgrace.

Shadpo:
We' re cited for our cruelty. Survival of the fittest is obscene!
To bite the hand that feeds you is a jungle law. It's nothing less than mean,
But at least we have more honesty than all the accusations which are hurled.
I wouldn't be a human. No, I couldn't be a human for the world!

Unicorn:
The lives of humans offer opportunities galore,
But there are worse perplexities than eating from the floor!
Although it would be nice to be in charge of lots of folks, I guess.

Grooboo:
And it would be nice to eat all I could hold, or more, or less.

Shadpo: And it would be nice to be so rich I'd never face distress.

All three:
And yet, I wouldn't be a human,
No, I couldn't be a human on a bet!

From *The Rise and Fall of the Girl* by Julian Rush

Chapter Four

I had to endure three days and two nights before the next Staff/Parish Relations meeting, so I made a decision to stay as calm as I could. Meditation had already been part of my life for quite a while, and I was accustomed to the routine. I felt more centered and aware of my direction when I meditated, and during that weekend, the practice significantly sharpened my insights about who I was and where I needed to go. I would sit in front of a burning candle trying to focus on the events that were swirling about me. I went through all the possibilities and alternatives I could conceive—what if "A" happens, if "B" happens, if "C" happens? I tried to examine every aspect of the situation. Instead of being Chicken Little, running around in panic crying, "the sky is falling, the sky is falling", I was withdrawing to a quiet place and deliberating about the condition of the sky. Was it indeed falling, and if so, what could I or would I do about it? I also sought to examine the bonding or alienation I felt with different individuals, find ways to overcome whatever alienation I could and increase bonding wherever possible.

During my therapy sessions with Anne, one of the issues that arose again and again was the importance of learning to trust my own process. As a result, in this crisis situation, I was making a clear, strong effort to be in contact with my own processing and as conscious as possible about who I was and the position I was in. Having faced the reality that I was a gay male, and having accepted that, I also knew I had been created this way.

Just recognizing that reality and affirming that fact had a cleansing effect I had never felt before. I had managed to fling that long-closed closet door wide open and free myself. I felt liberated, even free and strong. Despite the turmoil about me and within me, I was actually beginning to feel powerful. Paradoxically, I was feeling insecure about my professional future in the church, but I was able to begin imagining a future of promise and hope. There was a whirlwind around me, yet as I stood in the midst of the funnel, I felt at peace with myself and with God.

I was nervous about the Staff/Parish Relations meeting Sunday night, of course, but many of the committee members were nervous too, and consequently over-solicitous in welcoming me to the meeting. The group asked me to explain what it meant to be gay, how I had come to terms with this issue, and why I had chosen to tell anyone. This was followed by a question and answer period, in which people asked me questions.

"What makes you think you're gay?"

"Do you think you could change if you wanted to?"

"How can you live this long and then suddenly discover you're gay now?"

"How could you be quiet about this for so many years and then suddenly decide you have to tell everybody?"

"Why couldn't you just keep it a secret?"

"How can you be effective as a minister if people know you're gay?"

"How do you think parents would feel about their kids having a gay minister?"

"How do you think you can minister to people who can't accept you?"

"Don't you think homosexuality is wrong?"

The focus of this meeting was not only to find out about me and about gayness, but it also became a way for the individual members to let me know their thinking and to consider what the committee's next step would be. Those who were negative had made that quite obvious. But I could tell there were others who were struggling, trying to decide what was right, both for me and for everyone involved. The District Superintendent, who oversees area ministers, had joined us that evening, and he was unabashedly supportive, making no bones about communicating the Bishop's support as well. He made it clear that they both hoped First United Methodist Church of Boulder would find a way to keep me. The senior minister tried to play a neutral role by expressing no opinions and by making only clarifying comments. From the very beginning, he tried not to take sides, but that very caution proved to be problematic. Most of the people who felt strongly about the situation were in one of two groups, either faithfully for me or solidly against me. Because of their strong opinions, each group sought the support of the senior pastor. When he avoided taking a stand, he was severely criticized because neither group felt it had his support.

Before the meeting was over that night, I was asked to leave to enable the committee to deliberate in private. They did not intend to decide my future that night, but rather to determine how to de-escalate tensions and decide what the next steps should be. I felt calm during the meeting, and when it was over, I was very relieved. I too was also considering the next step and where it might lead. I was informed later that evening that the District Superintendent would be asked to request that Bishop Melvin Wheatley and the Cabinet strongly consider assigning me elsewhere as soon as possible. Meanwhile, I should remain in a visible, active ministry as long as I was serving First Methodist, Boulder. In addition, church-wide forums would be conducted, allowing people to ask questions and express opinions. Two would be conducted the following Sunday, one specifically for youth and another for adults.

I had only been restricted from appearing at the church until the Sunday night meeting, so Monday morning I went into my office as usual. I didn't stop at the downstairs office to chat, as was my habit. Not knowing how any of the staff members would react, I avoided the opportunity to find out. Shortly one secretary, then the other, came to my office and pledged their support. The staff had been told what was happening, and almost everyone was supportive. I chose to stay very busy the whole day, but found concentration hard. Most difficult was knowing that although many people knew, I had little idea who did and who didn't, or how those who knew would react.

The following Sunday evening the first congregational meeting for all the youth in the church was convened. With the exception of two families, both theologically conservative, the youth and their parents were overwhelmingly supportive. I knew the parents in one of the conservative families would have problems with my staying because of their negative stance on homosexuality, but when the boy himself stood up and spoke against me, I felt wounded. I had invested a great deal of time with him and his older brother and I was stunned that he could dismiss me so easily.

One of the most memorable moments of the entire process occurred during that first meeting. My twelve-year-old son stood up to speak on my behalf. During his speech he cried, but kept talking. The essence of his message was, "I can't understand why you are making such a big deal of this. My dad is still the same person he always was." I recall being seated across the room at the time, so I went over and sat by him. I leaned over and told him that I didn't care what happened after that. Having his support was worth it all.

> You can wander far from where you are.
> You can seek your fortune in distant places full of unknown faces
> You can search north, south or east and west,
> Up, down, below, above:
> It don't make no difference where you go.
> There ain't no place like love.
> Love is where you're cared for,
> Helped along and shared for.
> Love can stay on y'r trail wherever you roam.
> Love is where you're waited for,
> Where you're appreciated for the things you are.
> With love you're always home.

There ain't no place like love.
There ain't no place like love.
No, there ain't no place like love.

From *The Trials and Tribulations of Hank Cohen* by Julian Rush

The all-church meeting for adults followed, and most of the people were supportive. I was both surprised and grateful. Major issues of concern were (1) the opinions of other congregations if First Methodist kept a gay minister, (2) the possibility that parents would not bring their children to this church, and (3) the economic effect on the church when people left.

I realized quickly that for some people, the issue of homosexuality was so primal and deep that our five-year history together was simply wiped away. Homosexuality overrode not only our history together, but also any friendship that might have continued to exist. The rejection by some individuals was no surprise, but there were others who amazed me, whose Biblical perspective created an indifference to the time and life experiences we had shared over the years. It hurt deeply to think they could push me aside so easily.

Some dissatisfied church members exerted their influence outside of public settings. Late one afternoon I was invited to the home of a church couple to chat. The wife held a prominent position in the church, and our meeting began with her decision that we should pray together. She then told me that one of her best friends, of whom she was very fond, was lesbian. However, she pointed out, that friend is not a minister, and I should realize that my effective ministry in this church was over. "One of my best friends is gay, but..." In other words, the very best thing I could do for the congregation was resign and disappear. What might have been best for me was not a topic of the conversation.

I had already talked to the senior minister about the possibility of resigning, and I had even written out a resignation note and shown it to the

District Superintendent, John Nieves. John made it clear that I should definitely *not* resign. NO WAY! He and Bishop Wheatley and the Cabinet were committed to my staying on the staff of the church. They were of the opinion that with my background and years of experience serving that congregation, staying was within the realm of possibility. I was enormously affirmed to know that the Cabinet was behind me with such commitment.

With this counsel and encouragement, I decided not to resign. When some of the church leaders learned of this, there was consternation and displeasure, and they gathered support for a second all-church meeting which was scheduled for August 30, 1981. Some of these opponents thought that the first meeting had been lopsided and that expressions of support for me had been manipulated by my supporters and me. The second meeting turned out much as the first, with the majority of those who spoke being positive. At this point, it was decided that the congregation would meet with Bishop Wheatley and the Cabinet of District Superintendents.

A meeting of a local church with the Bishop and Cabinet was a major event in the life of any United Methodist congregation. The Cabinet was composed of six district superintendents representing the area served by the Rocky Mountain United Methodist Conference. These pastors would have to travel from their regions of service to Boulder for a one-night meeting. While three were from the Denver area, one was from Pueblo—more than one hundred miles away, another from Wyoming and a third from the western Colorado/Utah area. The calendars of all these pastors and the Bishop had to be adjusted to accommodate one evening, simply because one forty-five-year-old pastor finally acknowledged that he was gay.

There was one more calendar which was juggled that night—that of Phil Nash, a writer who was reporting for a weekly metropolitan Denver newspaper called *Westword*. Phil was the first writer to break the full story of the Boulder Church vs. the Gay Minister. His detailed story appeared in the October 29, 1981, issue of *Westword*, giving rise to a frenzy of publicity that soon became national. But that night, the story was still tucked away in the foothills of Boulder.

Bishop Wheatley and his wife, Lucille, were long-time champions of human rights. One of their three sons was gay, and they became major nurturers of the organization known as Parents and Friends of Lesbians and Gays. Over the years, the Bishop and the Cabinet (District Superintendents) had studied and deliberated about many human rights issues, including homosexuality. By the time my situation arose, much consciousness-raising had already taken place. The Bishop and the six Cabinet members were keenly aware of the human rights issues surrounding gays, and now the theories discussed earlier were coming to fruition with a genuine test case.

Over three hundred people gathered for the meeting that night. Seated in the front of the room were Bishop Wheatley, the Cabinet and our senior minister. I had discovered my older son in the audience and was sitting next to him in the back of the room. Two weeks later, when Phil Nash's story appeared, I relived some specific moments of that night and the events to follow.

The congregation of First United Methodist Church of Boulder wasted no time informing the Bishop that his decision must reflect the best interests of the church, which was characterized as a sinking ship. Rush's failure to disappear was considered a victory by his supporters; his lingering presence was anathema to those stern countenances of piety who felt his homosexuality disqualified him from the ministry. Others were irate that the church had come to a three-month standstill as it agonized over an issue it never wanted to confront.

Bishop Wheatley drew the meeting to order, outlining the process that had been followed in pursuing Rush's continuing relationship with the Church. Then he clarified church law: "Why is there not a clear unequivocal statement declaring homosexual persons ineligible for ordination? Because the 1980 General Conference decisively and explicitly voted down, not once, but twice—not one, but two separate and distinct resolutions that tried to do exactly that!"

The Bishop said that, although many would rather not face the realities of ambiguity in Church law and would prefer to eliminate homosexuality from the pulpit, his role was to bring a resolution that would least harm and most benefit all concerned. "Where the resources for excellence exist, mediocrity is a sin," he said.

The Bishop added that it was his responsibility to help preserve the integrity of a [United] Methodist minister who faced the end of a creative career spanning almost two decades.

[The] Head Pastor...sat in the front of the room with the Bishop and his cabinet of district supervisors. In addressing the congregation, he boomed: "Julian Rush and I are friends. Julian Rush and I disagree very strongly on whether or not a youth minister in the church can be a declared gay. That bothers me. That does not for one minute detract from my personal affection for Julian Rush."

Then [he] waved for Rush to join him at the front of the room. "I want to hear what Julian has to say."

Rush was unprepared. "I know some of you have a very hard time in a negative way just dealing with my presence here. And let me assure you I don't bear any hostility or bitterness. I've been with you people for five and a half years...and this is the most meaningful ministry I've had. You've been cordial, you've been kind, you've been considerate. I know this is not easy for you. Let me assure you it is not easy for me. At least whether we agree or disagree, we can still reach out and touch one another."

One by one, members of the church spoke.

A teen-age girl came to the microphone and chided the congregation for using the youth issue. She said the junior high youth didn't think Julian Rush's sexual preference made any difference and that there were no bad effects from their minister's influence over the past five years. "The only bad effect will be if you take Julian away from us."

A man in the rear of the room chided the Christian attitudes of church members who had lately been heard to say, "We love Julian, but..." The man continued, "I wonder if I might be the next to have certain conditions tied to your Christian love."

An adult youth worker in the church said that although he had often disagreed with Rush over the education of young people, "The crucial thing is that Julian makes Christ real for those kids and I think that's the basis for saying he's competent to continue."

A woman who had served as a member of the [Staff/Parish Relations] committee read extracts from letters expressing the negative concerns conveyed to her by many church members: "He should not try to give us the word of God, which he does not live up to himself." "His openness shall certainly draw other homos to our church." "Further future growth will be severely limited if it is known that a professed homo is ministering in violation of church law." "Since Julian has chosen a life style detrimental to marriage and the sanctity of the family, it has damaged our trust in him as a leader of our youth."

A young man, the president of the senior high group, said, "By getting rid of Julian, we are not getting rid of the problem. Julian fits no stereotype and never has. What kind of Christian attitude is it to get rid of Julian? One argument is that the Bible teaches that homosexuality is wrong. Does not the Bible also teach that women should obey their husbands?"

One of the church patriarchs held his piece until the very end, then delivered it in a dramatic pitch. "I am not a Biblical student, but I think I understand what I read. And I read into that Bible that homosexuality is wrong. And you people who are arguing here tonight for us to accept it are asking me to compromise my moral issues…my religious issues! And I don't believe I can. Julian, the solution is with you. If you want to save this church with the polarization that is here tonight, you must resign!"

Finally Bishop Wheatley announced he would conclude the meeting in fifteen minutes. The last to speak were the district supervisors, who had earlier informally but unanimously accorded Rush their full support.

The meeting ended without a decision and with more gossip in the parking lot of the Boulder First [United] Methodist Church.

On October 21, the [Staff/Parish Relations] committee, Rush, Bishop Wheatley, [the senior pastor], and others met to find an alternative for Rush. The options considered included complete termination, no termination, and several other ideas which might include part-time work at Boulder First [United] Methodist.

Reverend Julian Rush was completely terminated as of October 31. He will receive half pay for two months as severance, and he is prohibited from future work at First [United] Methodist of Boulder. Some of the proceedings of the meeting which led to this decision have been sealed by a gentlemen's agreement…

From *Westword*, October 29, 1981, pp 7,10

Phil's article did not include the last few blows to come my way before the fray was over. The meeting which decided the specific action the church was to take was convened for that purpose October 21, just as Phil noted. The primary question before the committee was, "Could the church somehow see its way to continue supporting the ministry of the Reverend Rush, even on a part-time basis?" The senior minister opened the proceedings that night by reading a letter he had brought with him. The content conveyed that due to current pressures and frustration, he was unable to continue in effective ministry at First Methodist Boulder and was resigning. For the next two and one-half hours, the conversation and focus of the committee was completely turned from what would happen to Julian to persuading the senior minister to reconsider. It was close to ten o'clock, after much expended energy, before the group focused on my situation again. After a very short deliberation, the group voted not to continue me in ministry at First United Methodist Church in Boulder.

The senior minister had effectively determined the outcome of the issue, bless his bones. The best that could be said was that I was undermined; the worst that I was sabotaged. In either case, I was defeated. Had all the processing the church done been useless? Was my five-year ministry—an effective one in the eyes of most—to end with "thanks a lot and out with the garbage?"

> How can a council of so-called intelligent people
> Decide on an action as drastic as this?
> Why should they try to determine the fate of those people
> with no preparation that something's amiss?
> Every flower grows in its own little garden,
> Protected from the world outside.
> Every flower knows only one small horizon—
> The sunlight overhead, its rich and earthy bed,
> The breezes and the gentle rains that fall:
> But the very same sun and the very same earth

And the same winds and raindrops should be shared
Among the flowers one and all.
From *Don't Take It So Hard, Mr. Johnson* by Julian Rush

I had entertained the possibility that I might be able to continue in ministry, at least in some way, but now the door was shut. I was out in the cold. There was no place to go. Even though the Bishop and Cabinet were supportive, they had nowhere to place me. I felt fear. Even that night I spent alone in the apartment during that first Staff/Parish Relations meeting, the panic had not been as strong as it was now. The questions were the same: Where will I go? What will I do? How will I survive? That earlier night I could still entertain possibility. Now I faced reality. I felt lost, betrayed, sick inside, and totally terrorized. In the action of a few minutes, everything I had done in ministry, all the education and training I worked through, all the relationships which had been built—all of that made no difference. A queer is a queer and that's that.

I began with expectations high
And goals sincere.
I felt replete with dreams that died
Before the world could hear.
Where did it go wrong for me?
It's the end of the song,
When the lights dim and the silence closes in.

From *JesusSong* by Julian Rush

The church members continued to process their own feelings. Much earlier, when *The Man Who Can Save the Day* and another musical play had been performed, there were discussions about sponsoring a workshop on homosexuality. Early in the current controversy, some of my supporters pushed even harder for such a conference, thinking that people could learn more and be able to dialogue with one another intelligently, rather than just standing up and swapping opinions. But the senior minister and some church officials feared that such a workshop would give rise to accusations that they were supporting me. Consequently, there was no informational input provided for a debate which would change my life and that of the church.

Whether I had been allowed to stay or not, the time together would have softened some hard feelings, and raised the consciousness level of the congregation. As it turned out, the conference on homosexuality was conducted, but not until the weekend following my dismissal. Too little, and much too late."

At the same time the church uproar was occurring, the finance committee had been preparing for the annual budget campaign. I was terminated in late October; and the campaign began in November. The success and viability of the church's operations depended on a good fund drive. For planning the next year's salaries, plus operational and denominational expenses, the church needed to know what financial support could be expected.

Those who objected to the action of the church to dismiss me were suffering disillusionment, disenchantment and utter frustration.

"How can someone who has been in ministry here over five years be quietly slipped into a garbage bag and shoved inconspicuously through the back door?"

"How can a church that talks about love do this?"

"We shouldn't tolerate this, but what in the world can we do about it?"

On the other side were the people who were quite relieved when the decision was made that I would leave. Now they could get back to normal; get on with it again. Those who were actively involved with the finance campaign evidenced a feeling of both frustration and urgency. I had decided not to disappear on October 31, but continue to tie up loose strings for those who would follow. Since the church was not planning to hire anyone to replace me right away, I assumed I had ample time to pack.

The senior minister, however, always the good scout, informed me that my office would be needed. The next day I packed without sorting anything.

> We knew what we needed
> And thought we had succeeded
> To realize our dream we knew how.
> But our inspiration
> Has ended in frustration.
> Where is that paradise now?
> Bewildered and stranded,
> We work on single-handed
> To try to face the future somehow.
> But our inspiration
> Has ended in frustration.
> Where is that paradise now?

From *On Friday With the Bluejays* by Julian Rush

There were members of the church who insisted on a goodbye reception, and an official committee was set up to orchestrate the event. The irony was impossible to ignore: A congregation that wouldn't allow me to stay would give me a send-off. I didn't want a reception (a word which literally means the act of receiving); the idea was awkward and meaningless. If anyone wanted to say anything to me, they could do it on an individual basis. The senior minister again prevailed, however, pointing out that a number of people needed to express their goodbyes and thank you's. I went along with it, but still remember the event as being very stiff and awkward for all concerned.

Throughout the weeks ahead there were occasional rays of sunlight. One woman in the congregation had come to my office and her message was clear, "I've always felt that being gay was wrong. I've been taught all my life that there was something wrong with people who are gay. But during the last five years, I have come to know you as a person, and you don't fit any of the stereotypes. Because of you, I'm having to reassess my ideas and feeling about gayness."

A grandmother in the church also came to me in the midst of the foray. She expressed her sadness that I was going through so much, and I assured her that I had been surrounded by positive supporters like herself.. She revealed to me that she had a grandson, a grown man, who suffered the loss of two jobs and a great deal of tragedy and heartache in his life because he was gay. She said I had given both her and her grandson new hope.

The last day I was officially employed by the Boulder church, I went alone into the sanctuary and stood in the pulpit. I felt that I needed to ritualize the finish of it all. There was a distinct possibility that I might not ever stand in a pulpit as a *bona fide* minister again.

It was mid-morning on a weekday, and the sun was shining through all of the multi-colored glass cubes on the south side of the sanctuary, bathing the room in a rainbow of colors. I had expected the moment to be sad, but as I stood there in the sunlight, I felt a real sense of celebration, a oneness with the universe. I was moving into a new creative dynamic where I had never lived before. What I was doing was absolutely right for me.

Chapter Five

Phil:
There is no task that's easy;
No longer a time that's slow;
There is no land, except in dreams,
Where peaceful waters flow.

From *On Friday With The Blue Jays* by Julian Rush

Within a month, Bishop Melvin E. Wheatley, leader of the United Methodist Church in Colorado, southern Wyoming, and Utah, sent the following letter to the ministers of the region:

November 20, 1981

"Dear Clergy Colleague of the Rocky Mountain Conference:

"This letter is offered to update you on the latest developments pertaining to Julian Rush's appointment. As of Sunday, November 8, your Appointive Cabinet's consultation with the pastor and people of St. Paul's United Methodist Church of Denver and with Julian Rush was completed. On the basis of that consultation, I am appointing Julian Rush associate pastor at St. Paul's as Minister of Community Concerns. Though Julian has already begun relating to the St. Paul's congregation and George Christie, and he has begun to design their shared ministries, the official dating of the appointment will be as of December 1, 1981. The percentage of full-time appointment possible in this new assignment will be determined by the financial resources available to support it.

"To questions raised as to the Disciplinary basis for this appointment of a pastor who has identified his sexual orientation as same sex, I offer my own interpretations and understandings in response....

"Do I believe that homosexuality is a sin?

"I am an enthusiastically heterosexual male. Is my heterosexuality a virtue, a sign of righteousness, an accomplishment or victory of some kind on my part? Of course not. I had nothing whatsoever to do with my *being* heterosexual. My sexual orientation is a mysterious gift of God's grace, communicated through an exceedingly complex set of chemical, biological, chromosomal, hormonal, environmental, developmental factors totally outside my control. My heterosexuality is a gift—neither a virtue nor a sin. What I do with my heterosexuality, however, *is* my personal, moral and spiritual responsibility. My *behavior* as heterosexual, therefore, may be very sinful—brutal, exploitive, selfish, promiscuous, superficial. My behavior as a heterosexual may on the other hand be beautiful—tender, considerate, loyal, other-centered, profound.

"Precisely the same distinction between *being* homosexual and *behaving* as a homosexual applies as to heterosexuals. Homosexuality quite like heterosexuality is neither a virtue nor an accomplishment. Homosexual orientation is a mysterious gift of God's grace communicated through an exceedingly complex set of chemical, biological, chromosomal, hormonal, environmental, developmental factors totally outside my homosexual friends' control. Their homosexuality is a gift, neither a virtue nor a sin. What they do with their homosexuality, however, is definitely their personal, moral and spiritual responsibility. Their behavior as homosexuals may be very sinful—brutal, exploitive, selfish, promiscuous, superficial. Their behavior as homosexuals, on the other hand, may be beautiful—tender, considerate, loyal, other-centered, profound.

"With this interpretation of the mystery that must be attributed to both heterosexual and homosexual orientations, I clearly do not believe that homosexuality is a sin.

"Do I then believe that a declared homosexual person should be appointed as a pastor of a church?

"I do not think an avowed *heterosexual* should be appointed as a pastor of a church—if that's all I know about him or her. For the fact of heterosexuality tells me nothing whatsoever about the person's character, temper, behavior, honesty, morality much less about the clarity of the person's calling of God, commitment to Jesus Christ as Savior and Lord and endowment with sufficient supply of gifts and graces and fruits of the Holy Spirit to function as a representative minister in the church.

"Just so, if all I know about a person is that that person's sexual orientation is same sex rather than other sex, that tells me absolutely nothing just of itself as to that person's dependability, honesty, kindness, truthfulness, cruelty or compassion, much less anything about that person's clarity of calling by God to preach the Gospel, commitment to Jesus Christ as Savior and Lord, and endowment with sufficient supply of gifts and graces and fruits of the Holy Spirit to function as a representative minister in the church.

"In other words, the Biblical, traditional and ecclesiastical trinity of criteria to test qualification for appointment as a pastor: (1) authentic call of God; (2) unequivocal commitment to Jesus Christ; (3) gifts, graces and fruits of the Holy Spirit—have nothing to do with sexual orientation.

"Many heterosexuals obviously do not pass the [above] trinitarian test. Some homosexuals just as obviously do pass those tests. Those persons of same sex orientation who do pass the tests should be appointed to parishes subject to exactly the same dual tests of living under God's sovereignty and in beneficial love and charity with neighbors as heterosexuals are subject to.

"Whatever gradations of agreement or disagreement you and I may share on these particular issues, we are under orders from our Master, and as colleagues, to do all within our respective powers to maximize our mutual understanding and to press forward in our individual collective ministries. Let us strenuously work and fervently pray for just such pilgrims' progress in Jesus' name. To that end this letter is shared with you.

"Cordially,
Melvin E. Wheatley"

If the newspapers had shown remarkable interest in my plight to this point, the coverage had only begun. Less than two years earlier, the United Methodist Church had been embroiled in a controversy regarding homosexuality that had not yet cooled when the Bishop moved decisively on my behalf. A woman employed over five years with the national staff of the Woman's Division of the United Methodist Board of Global Ministries had acknowledged she was lesbian. When she tendered her resignation, she was encouraged to stay, and did so. A United Methodist uproar ensued, and she was fired. That caused more controversy and more headlines. The following year at the 1980 General Conference of the United Methodist Church, a national event scheduled once every four years, lively discussions about the church's social principles occupied the headlines. That year, Ellen Clark, a leader of the United Methodist lesbian and gay caucus called Affirmation, briefly described to the weekly *The United Methodist Reporter* the history of the issue over the last few years:

> In 1972 [United Methodist General Conference] when this subject came up, there was panic and near hysteria to put it down. In 1976 the people began to understand the issue. Now [in 1980] a quarter of the general Conference was willing to stand up and be counted. I think that is significant.

It was indeed significant, and newsworthy, to radio, television and the press. By appointing me to another church, Melvin E. Wheatley, the

Bishop of Colorado, Wyoming, Montana and Utah, had stepped squarely into the fire.

The Boulder *Daily Camera*, the *Rocky Mountain News*, and *The Denver Post* all ran extensive stories as the reaction to the Bishop's stand reverberated throughout United Methodism. Of course *The United Methodist Reporter* was deluged with articles, columns and letters for both the national and local editions. Two churches within the Rocky Mountain Conference called for the resignation of their Bishop. Ironically, one of them was not only one of the largest United Methodist Churches in the western United States, but also the church where I was youth pastor just a few years before, First United Methodist Church of Colorado Springs.

By April of 1982, accusations of heresy were filed against the Bishop by a Georgia minister and eighty-nine of his church members. Under United Methodist law, this required an appointed group of ministers to render a decision on whether or not there were sufficient grounds to bring formal charges of heresy and therefore require a church trial. Meanwhile, the ramifications of my story had stirred enough interest that a reporter from *The New Yorker*, Calvin Trillin, was sent to do a lengthy article on me that was published in January. In May, headline attention shifted to the National Council of Churches as it grappled with an application by the Universal Fellowship of Metropolitan Community Churches to become a member of the Council. Since the UFMCC denomination served primarily the lesbian and gay community, journalists jumped right from a United Methodist Bishop's heresy accusations regarding homosexuality to the much wider sphere of the National Council of Churches and homosexuality. The story had come a long way from a Staff/Parish Relations committee meeting one night in a United Methodist Church in Colorado less than a year earlier.

Such persistent coverage began to involve many who had hoped I would drop out of sight and that the Bishop would endorse my disappearance. Below is of one of the letters received by the Bishop during this period.

"As a former member of 1st Meth. here—Colo. Springs, at that time Julian was serving under Dr. Laroue [Lacour] and Bob Tuttle. As a professing born again Christian God has burden my heart. To write both of you are ministers who have attended well known Methodist Colleges of Theology. It is very distressing, for God's Word has not changed, if you add one word or take one word, God's judgment is sure "Vengance is mine", thus says the Lord. In Old Testament why did God destroy Sodom and Gommorah? Sexal Sins, Sodomy. It was wrong then, It is wrong now. Read Romans Chp 1. Start at Verse 22 to get the complete context (King James) through Verse 32, then go back to Verse 27 – it might be well to implant the message on your heart that you Sin not.

"It is sin here, and not any man of God who participates in such behavior can not be a candidate for God's ministry. Julian I'm shocked…. I believe now that you are in need of mental therapy. As for you Dr. Wheatley, are you, a man of your ministerial experience, trying to compromise with the Devil? Well I have news for you. God is not a man to compromise if you have not learned. You better return to a school of sound theology. I grew up in the Methodist Ep. Church South as did Julian…. I know for certain it was not approved. I do not know where you grew up. Dr. Wheatley you have used poor judgment in this appointment.

"This practice is Sin, not any man of God who is preaching the Word should be recognized in the Methodist faith, or be allowed to fill a pulpit for serve in leadership. I'm sorry Julian, but there is hope for you by the saving blood of Christ. If you really desire to turn from this sinful practice and sincerely turn to God seeking His God's help, He will answer your plea. It may be tough at first, but, think how free and clean your entire soul will become as God through the Holy Spirit cleanses you…. Can you realize how the youth that you once directed in the former charges may feel. May God's still small voice be heard and lead you and you be submissive is my prayer to forsaking such a sinful behavior.

"As for you Dr. Wheatley, God's will be done in dealing with you and this outrageous appointment.

"Julian I'm sure you remember my daughter as she and your son were friends. I'm praying for you."

> You have to be stopped.
> You're obsessed with this lunacy,
> Blinded by zealots who foster the "way."
> You have to be stopped.
> You are bound for destruction now
> Unless you can conquer these dreams of decay.
> You have to be stopped,
> At whatever the sacrifice, simple discomfort, or strife.
> You have to be stopped
> For whatever the outcome:
> Your change, your repentance, your Life!

From *P.T. Was Here* by Julian Rush

Alexandria:
Look at me, yes, at me!
Not at my eyes, or my lips or my hair.
Look at me!
Don't act like you're listening to words you can't hear;
Don't skim on my surface and call it sincere.
Look at me, look at me, look at me.

Look at me, yes, at me!
Not at my body or even my face.
Look at me! Your earnest attention is only veneer.
My feelings are crying for someone to hear.
Look at me, look at me, look at me!

You claim you're concerned. Well, forget it.

Your efforts are terribly small.
I don't want your friendship *au gratin*.
I'd rather have nothing at all.

Look at me, yes, at me!
Not at the way I walk or I talk
Look at me!
You're looking straight at me, but what do you see?
The image of something you want me to be?
Well, for God's sake, just listen! For once hear my plea.
Look at me!

From *The Rise And Fall of The Girl* by Julian Rush

Before the letters started coming, the opposition had been verbal. Below are some of the comments made to me in Boulder.

One woman: "I really respect you, but I don't agree with you are doing. If you stay here, it will split the church, and I think we must make sure that the church stays intact, no matter what."

Another woman: "I still love you and care about you, but I just can't let you be a minister anymore."

The senior minister's wife: "I don't know who you think you are. Why couldn't you just resign quietly and get the hell out of here? Why do you have to stir everything up this way? Do you have some kind of a Jesus complex? What do you think you're going to prove by splitting the whole church?"

And then from a fellow church worker: "I can't see how you're doing this to your kids. If you had any respect for them, you'd just resign and leave quietly and avoid all the publicity. You're not thinking of them at all."

Not long after the news broke across the country, I received a call from the younger daughter of a family in Fort Worth, Texas. All three of the children had been involved in the plays we produced there, and I had built and maintained a deep friendship with the family. I visited them every time I went through Fort Worth, and had stayed overnight at their home. The daughter was calling to assure me of her support, but I never heard from the rest of the family. Recently, the father and mother had become disenchanted with the liberal minister at First United Methodist Church in Fort Worth, and had joined a small Baptist Church. I could assume the reasons for their silence.

When the media blitz began, I wrote a letter to a very close friend from college. My last year in college was extremely difficult, and he was a freshman who was present and caring for me during a time when I had a nervous collapse. What I realize now is that I was trying to deal with the reality of being gay by pushing it so far down that it could never surface again. But at the time, I didn't understand. I only knew that he had been present for me. I wrote him to thank him for all he had done. He never responded.

It was painful when people I assumed to be accepting and supportive surprised me by distancing themselves or actively pushing me away. When I went to my son's high school for a concert or play, I never looked around me. During intermission I just remained in my seat because I assumed there were people there who didn't want to recognize me. I'm sure some of that was in my own head, but I'm also just as sure some of it wasn't.

When I went to my two son's soccer games, parents with whom I had a speaking acquaintance in the past were there, but few of them recognized my presence. One could assume that they were intent on the game and since I didn't go right up to them and initiate a conversation, it was no big deal. But there was an obvious attempt by some to avoid me.

When I went to the Bishop's Christmas Conference at Park Hill United Methodist Church in Denver, I felt the same way. Walking into the church was uncomfortable. I had been Youth Pastor there many years before and I knew there were people from that era who would rather I not be there. At such times, I was able to imagine how a black person must feel in an almost all-white group; even if you yourself didn't feel different, there are people present who think you are.

I had read about this phenomenon in literature written by blacks, but I think actual experience is the only way it can be understood. The atmosphere is unmistakable; not at all the same as being paranoid, assuming all people out there are against you. There are subtleties involved, subtleties of which I have become acutely aware over time. I observe people going out of their way to avoid me, all the while appearing to be so focused on something else that they don't see me.

At a recent United Methodist ministers' conference, I was talking with a woman pastor. In the midst of our conversation, a male minister, obviously not one of my supporters, walked up and began talking with her, never once recognizing that I was present. Sometimes I need to tell myself that, by God, I deserve to be there as much as anyone!

> A hurt that's on the outside is the easier by far,
> Since it heals so very quickly and, at worst, may leave a scar.
> And the hurt that's on the inside will eventually wane,
> Tho the heart will still remember all the tears and
> All the pain.
> So that we will not forget too soon
> How we felt in all the fuss,
> So that we will do for others
> What we'd have them do for us.
> The hurt that's on outside goes as quickly as a chime,
> But the hurt that's on the inside takes a long, long time.

From *The Resurrection Thing* by Julian Rush

Despite all the negative reaction, I had been appointed (without salary) to St. Paul's United Methodist Church in Denver. Prior to the blowup in Boulder, St. Paul's had made a decision to undertake a new direction in ministry by reaching out to singles, elderly, and lesbian and gay persons in the neighborhood. When I was terminated in Boulder, the St. Paul's pastor,

Rev. George Christie, and the Bishop had conferred about requesting the Staff/Parish Relations committee at St. Paul's to accept a transfer of my appointment. At the Bishop's recommendation, I met with the committee.

A couple in the group had a son who, as a young boy, had apparently experienced a negative encounter with a gay male. They were unalterably opposed to me. However, everyone else was supportive, and I was appointed to St. Paul's as an Associate Pastor. After that night, the couple left St. Paul's and never returned.

Even though the staff position was created to enable me to remain in the United Methodist connectional system, I attended St. Paul's regularly on Sundays, playing piano, helping to lead worship, and occasionally preaching.

Meanwhile, all was not settled in Boulder. While some of my supporters had resigned themselves to the realities, others were determined not to let go.

> *Peter:*
> We had all given up
> We were sure the group was finished
> When they crucified our leader on the hill outside of town
> But you can't stop truth!
>
> *Group:*
> No, you can't stop truth!
>
> *Peter:*
> And you can't
>
> *Group:*
> No, you can't
>
> *Peter:*
> Oh, you can't

Group:
No you can't

Peter:
No, you can't keep a good man down!

From *JesusSong* by Julian Rush

There were many people like Nani Schenk, a mother and a member of the church, who was quoted in the Boulder *Daily Camera*:

> I am for Julian 100 percent. I worked with Julian as youth choir director, I've been on two tours with Julian, and I watched him work with kids and adults. He does a beautiful job with them.

One of the former youth parents, a lawyer named Bill Love, invited me to lunch and suggested the idea of a house church. He was a parent of both a son and daughter in the youth department and was very committed to my staying in ministry. At first the idea appealed to me. Here was an unexpected opportunity to participate in a creative church group. But, growing wiser and more cautious now, I considered the potential political fallout.

There were already highly charged feelings among the church members, and forming a house church could be interpreted as divisive, as if I were trying to siphon away members from First Methodist. Bill understood my hesitance, but challenged my resistance by joining with others who shared his view, and they paid a visit to the Bishop.

When Bill and I met again, he advised me that Bishop Wheatley had approved the idea. The Bishop's position was that a house church would be no problem as long as worship services were not held at a time that would compete with First Methodist or any other church. When I was told the group had gone to the Bishop, I was excited, and my enthusiasm grew. A nucleus of people began to meet, and the Bishop attended the first meeting. We obviously had his full support, and through the dialogue process we began to work on a structure. We made a list of those we knew were disenchanted with the current situation, and they were polled regarding the amount of money they would be willing to pledge if a house church were formed. There was adequate financial support pledged for a part-time salary and running expenses, so the church was formed, officers were chosen, a bank account was opened and a budget adopted, all in about a month. One couple volunteered to coordinate the process, and we decided to meet in homes.

A large number of house church participants were parents of youth with whom I had worked. Others were people I had worked with in church leadership positions. The factor that united the group seemed to be the conviction that the outcome of my situation at the First Methodist of Boulder was untenable. If the house church didn't accomplish anything else, some of these people who desperately wanted to be part of a viable ministry of the church were able to continue in a fashion they could accept. Some had also gathered because they wanted me to have a viable ministry. But these emphases of the group faded quickly. We discovered together the exciting possibilities that lay before us in being a real honest-to-God church with no limitations. We were literally free to be whomever and whatever we chose to be.

> Yes, we're together again. Oh yeah!
> And we will savor
> The chance to revitalize our spirits again, and when
> The time has arrived to be separate once more, then
> We'll take our memories.
> Yes, we're together again, oh yeah,
> For we belong together.

From *The Man Who Could Save The Day* by Julian Rush

House church members were active participants in leading worship, including the children and youth. This was a highly involved group—lots of people and lots of energy. Meeting in homes became difficult, so the governing committee found an ecumenical building close to the University of Colorado (CU) campus in which we could rent an office, and thereby gain weekly use of the chapel for our Sunday afternoon meeting. Originally, we gathered only as a worshiping community, but moving into the building enabled us to initiate educational opportunities as well.

Once a month we shared a potluck together, and we soon became a genuine community. We also shared with the members of St. Paul's, and on at least two occasions, some house church members traveled to Denver to worship.

Our house church was unusual in one aspect. Most Methodist congregations had communion only once a month, but we shared communion every Sunday. At first there were people who resisted my idea of weekly communion, but they became more comfortable as we began to process the experience and became more informal in the liturgy. People would come forward in small groups, and after offering the bread and wine (or grape juice for those who wished) we dipped the bread in the wine and members of the group served each other. When each had been served, the entire group embraced and one person prayed on behalf of everyone. After a few weeks of communion shared in this intensely personal way, weekly communion was valued even by those who had resisted.

My role as minister of the house church included structuring and leading the worship service on Sunday afternoons and maintaining reasonable ongoing contact with the members. If persons were missing for a couple of Sundays, I would follow up to see how they were doing. One of the most difficult aspects of that period of time for me was producing a sermon weekly. While I didn't realize what was happening until much later, I was processing an enormously painful experience, and I was experiencing increasing difficulty coming up with what I wanted to say. In previous sermon settings I could always speak in a relevant way in any situation. Now I found myself returning to the same themes. Because I felt such a strong obligation to help heal the rift between some of the people in the house church and First Methodist, my topics typically included forgiveness, understanding, and going the second mile. Finally, I began feeling that my sermons were same song, fifth verse. I responded by placing less emphasis on the sermon and more on the liturgy.

At the same time I was working with the house church and St. Paul's, I found a 40-hour-a-week job as well. The City and County of Denver sponsored an agency called Chrysalis, which offered alternate options and opportunities for young people involved in prostitution. Before the Chrysalis job came through, I had taken temporary work. For a short while I held a job with an electronics firm. For the first time in my life I had to punch a time clock, but at least a little cash was flowing in. In addition, Doug McKee, the CU campus Methodist minister, offered me a janitorial job at the Wesley Foundation building. The income from the custodial work and the electronics job helped me survive until January, when the Chrysalis job began.

I was beginning to recover and stabilize. I was still seeing Anne Schaef, my therapist, and continued to spend thirty to forty-five minutes each morning meditating, which helped me to center and balance myself. Things were coming together, and I was surrounded by supportive people.

While I was looking for work, I always felt frightened when I entered a place of business to deliver my resume or interview for a job. I felt vulnerable, and the hurt and anger would well up in me and I would ask myself again, "Why am I having to do this?"

By contrast, the interview at St. Paul's with the Bishop and the Staff/Parish Relations committee was extremely comfortable. I was confident. I knew what I could bring to St. Paul's, and I was on familiar turf.

When I began the custodial job at the Wesley Foundation, I was grateful for the money, but I had never worked at what I perceived at the time to be a menial job. I resented having to mop floors and scrub johns to survive. When I was working alone, there was no problem, but whenever students were around, I felt awkward. One day a member of my former youth group at First Methodist walked in. He was horrified to see his former youth minister working as a custodian. I was embarrassed but also amused at his reaction.

While I was employed as a temporary at Resource Electronics, my responsibility was to phone prospective clients to interest them in purchasing circuit boards. I didn't know a circuit board from a banana, and people frequently asked questions I could not answer. The work was rote, the minutes dragged, and the days seemed endless. I only worked there three weeks, but those were some of the longest weeks of my life. After the first week there, I learned that Chrysalis had accepted me for the youth worker position, which gave me something to look forward to.

All through my upheaval, I never felt God was punishing me for anything. Theologically, I have never bought into the idea that if bad things happen to you then God is punishing you, and if good things happen God is rewarding you. Neither my seminary studies nor my personal experience bore out that belief. I have known people—good solid Christian people—to whom very bad things have happened. I have also known some quintessential nerds who had extremely good fortune in their lives. In my case, for every bad thing that happened, there were new doors opening. I don't believe God pushes me in a particular direction, but rather opens many doors, and offers me multiple choices. The choices I made during this time were not the only choices available, just the ones that looked best. To be led by the Spirit is a risky and frightening business, but I believe that I act on my knees, and I don't ever really know whether a decision is going to be right or wrong. While I could have interpreted my decision to acknowledge my gayness as a wrong decision, I now believe that what I did was right. Through the whole process, I felt centered, and in tune with what I was doing and where I was going.

There were also external events that served to reinforce me. Often these came in the form of people seeking me out to tell me how my story had significantly influenced their lives. Sometimes there was an unexpected phone call or an unsolicited letter. One call came from a Methodist minister in Alabama who thanked me for "doing this for all of us." He indicated there was no way he could stand up and be counted. He was sure there were a lot of closeted gay ministers like himself all over the country, but having one person stand firm and take the heat certainly gave others hope. He was convinced such a stand would help create long-range changes for the Church at large. One of the most moving letters was written by a person who could not sign his name:

"Rev. Julian Rush

"It is with the most avid interest and unmitigated awe that I continue to follow the history of your unfaltering determination to pursue your chosen calling. This despite the tumultuous obstacle-laden course it has taken because society's ignorance and fear have forced the homosexual into a position of scorn and rejection. In their narrow-mindedness, they have us all categorized and stereotyped, little realizing that there are many who do not fit their picture of us, and not cognizant of the fact that even we resent the image that some activists of the community have given the whole subculture.

"Yes, I am a covert, non-practicing, very deeply closeted gay. I reached the age of puberty and sexuality during an era when homosexuality was never mentioned, much less discussed. The impact of realizing that I belonged to a group totally ostracized and banished from society, much like the lepers of old, left me no choice but to carry this onus deep within myself. I had absolutely no recourse to anyone who might offer some measure of solace, advice or consolation, fearing that by discussing it with family, friends or even the minister of the faith I then professed, I would suffer the rejection I so badly feared at a time of life when acceptance is paramount.

"I am in my early sixties and have been forced, out of fear of discovery and subsequent exposure, to carry this burden with no outside support or encouragement that would have been so helpful. I have accepted my homosexuality and refuse to wallow in a pool of self-pity, having found that such a lifestyle was only self-defeating and destructive emotionally and psychologically.

"I am in a profession that has earned me a goodly amount of esteem and respect from family and friends as well as those who make use of my services. On the other side of the coin, I belong to a group of our society in which youth and attractiveness are most essential. If a person has not established a one-on-one relationship with another gay by the time he has reached middle age or better, then, in reality, he has nothing to gain by revealing his true leanings. Since I cannot lay claim to either of these conditions, I feel I must remain in my closet. Exposure at this point in this time of my life would be anathema to my professional career, my family ties, and the regard of my friends.

"Fortunately, I have made the acquaintance of four gay men. They are active, albeit discreetly, in the gay community and so I find myself seeing but little of them. Between their careers and their social activities, they are kept busy to the point that I refuse to impose myself on their schedules lest I become a 'persona non grata'.

"Although they are most supportive of me and a great benefit to my sagging morale, I still find myself searching for what I need most, and have needed for some time, someone to whom I can turn, when, like everyone, I feel the need to vent that which is chewing on me so badly.

"As a result, I find myself turning to a much more solitary lifestyle, a direct antithesis to that to which I am accustomed. I can no longer put on the façade of being a well-adjusted single hetero male enjoying nothing but heterosexual company. I crave so badly the company of men of some refinement who share the same sexual orientation as I.

"Now that homosexuality is more freely discussed, the knife digs deepest when, at social functions, the topic is broached. It is then discussed and handled in a manner of derision and hatred, coupled with ribald, demeaning jokes and always accompanied by sneers and contempt. It is when the venom of the conversation reaches its zenith that I weep bitter tears at their ignorance and unchristianity deep inside until I can get alone and shed them openly.

"As I have stated, I have totally accepted the fact that I am gay. I do not resent my being gay, but I do resent the fact that our culture has relegated us to a position of not being accepted. Since I feel that I have nothing to offer, and hence, nothing to gain by coming out to any degree, I have decided that my only recourse is to remain as deeply closeted as I have been for so many years.

"I would give anything to have just one person, such as yourself, to whom I might turn when the load gets too heavy to bear alone. If this is living, then I can truly say, "Death, where is thy sting?" Lucky are they who have an outlet to unburden their innermost feelings as the need arises. I am most happy to read you have found the inner peace we all seek. I hope the Good Lord stays by your side lest you falter in your determination and mission to bring solace to those who need it so badly in a society that rejects us as it does.

"I wish I could have the opportunity and privilege of meeting someone like you personally. It [would] be a great help in overcoming the hardships crowding a very bleak world—that of the lonely closeted gay.

"I must apologize for the length of this letter, but please know that it has afforded me some relief to come even this closely to bringing to light that which has plagued me for so many years.

"Again, I hope the Good Lord continues to afford you the fortitude to continue the course you have chosen and that you continue to extend a helping hand to those fortunate enough to have access to your council.

"Keep up your sorely needed mission and God Bless.

"[signed] One who admires you and prays for your continued peace of mind.

*　　　　　*　　　　　*

Priestess:
Sing me a song of freedom.
Let it resound through all the dark corners
Where the suffering people cry in pain.
Sing me a song of freedom.
Let it abound in all those forgotten
Hearts where tragedy's scars may still remain.
In every land where hungry people languish,
Or human bondage may still be found,
For every soulful yearning for affection,
May all the loving voices sound together.
Sing me a song of freedom.
Let it surround the forces of darkness,
Driving forth with a jubilant refrain.
Sing me a song of freedom,
A song of freedom,
A song of freedom again.

From *The Rise And Fall of The Girl* by Julian Rush

Chapter Six

I reach out to you and you reach
Out to me across the space that
Separates and keeps our hands from touching.
Love comes slowly.
Love comes hard.
We move cautiously along the
Road where people come and go,
Reluctant to encounter one another.
Love comes slowly.
Love comes hard.
Why must I sit alone and ache inside with
Loneliness when here beside me
You sit just as sorrowful,
Pretending all is well yet wanting me?
Should I venture forth and reach my
Hand to yours and tell you that I
Care, would you be able to accept me?
Love comes slowly.
Love comes hard.

From *JesusSong* by Julian Rush

There was one more event that took place during the upheaval. On October 31, my last day at First United Methodist Church in Boulder, I met Larry. His home was in Kansas, but he was spending a couple of days at a friend's home in Denver. While there, Larry's friend had shown him some of the newspaper clippings about me. Despite Larry's disinterest in the organized church, something about the articles intrigued him enough that he mentioned he would like to meet me, and a get-together was arranged.

At that time of my life, I was not seeking a relationship, yet during the two hours we spent together, I felt drawn to Larry. After I left, I created an excuse to go back. When I returned, Larry and I were able to talk again for another hour, and something passed between us which we both recognized.

A few days later Larry's friend gave me a note which revealed that Larry felt very drawn to me and wished it were possible for us to meet again. I had already been thinking about writing him, so I sent a reply telling him basically the same thing. At that point, I don't think either of us expected anything significant to come of the letters. He was in Kansas, I was in Denver, and there was little possibility of anything else. However, because of my letter and the phone numbers I enclosed, he called to invite me to Kansas for Thanksgiving.

I remember the visit to Kansas as very intense and concentrated. We both seemed to be trying to tell the other everything about ourselves in the shortest time possible. We both happened to be wearing a ring, and before the weekend was over, we exchanged our rings. We couldn't know where the relationship might lead or whether there would be a future for us at all, but we were in agreement that what was between us at that moment was too good to ignore. We committed ourselves to each other for whatever might unfold, if indeed anything would, and decided to visit each other about once every six weeks, either in Kansas or in Denver, and see what happened. Frankly, exchanging the rings seemed a bit frightening and foolhardy to both of us at the time, but we went ahead anyway.

Before and after the Thanksgiving visit, there was a plethora of letters exchanged, with much communication on both the feeling and idea levels. Because we were so intentional about our sharing, we learned a great deal about each other in a short time. As the months passed, both of us realized we did not want to turn loose of the relationship. Our together-ness was very real, albeit geographically unsolved.

Between Thanksgiving and Christmas 1981, I began to wonder if Larry could find a way to move to Denver, or if perhaps I could entertain the possibility of a move to Kansas. By now, the house church was flourishing, even though I didn't feel capable of leading. Although I tried to put up a good front, I had been physically, emotionally, and spiritually diminished by the experience at First Methodist, and I knew I was faltering. Coming up with sermons to preach every Sunday became more and more difficult, and my energy was seriously lacking. But how could I leave this group? And how could I leave my sons?

I was also afraid of an unknown future with Larry. How could I know, in such a brief number of visits, whether the relationship could last?

There were some compelling reasons for getting out of Denver. Thousands of words on radio, TV and in the newspapers crowded the lives of my children and myself. My photograph was rerun regularly. In January the four-page story was published in *The New Yorker* and I became a national property. There was no getting used to the publicity; it was overwhelming to me and I wanted to release myself and my sons from the grip of reporters and the public eye.

By now I was working forty hours a week for Chrysalis, but due to ten-tative funding, there was no assurance that the position would last. On the other hand, Larry's job at the university in Emporia was secure. I was still participating in services at St. Paul's in Denver on Sunday mornings and conducting the house church Sunday afternoons in Boulder. Some ele-ments of the United Methodist Church threatened a heresy trial of Bishop Wheatley, for his support of me. As pressures intensified, the idea of leav-ing the turmoil seemed more and more appealing.

> If, upon examination
> You discover your frustration
> Stems from unexplainable confusion,

When your simple occupation
Grows into an irritation,
Making troubles gather in profusion,
Go down to Jerusalem.
Go down to Jerusalem.
Why don'cha go, go down to Jerusalem?
Go down to Jerusalem and leave it all behind.

From *P.T. Was Here* by Julian Rush

After thinking, talking, praying and agonizing for several months, my decision became clear: I would move to Kansas. Early in May of 1982, the house church came together for their last service as a worshiping group. The communion shared that day was highly charged because we realized that we had, together, touched the genuine essence of what the Church ought to be. Our time together had been very meaningful for all of the people there. In addition, this was the last day of a visit to Denver by Larry, and he would be leaving directly from the service to catch a plane back to Kansas. These were the last two hours we would see each other before I moved to Kansas in June.

I had designed an adaptation of John Wesley's love feast. In the front of the room on a table were two large pitchers, one full of water and one empty, and a large number of cups. There was also a loaf of bread. As each small group came forward, they would break bread together, share it, and then pour water from the full pitcher into a cup and share it. Whatever water was left in the cup would be poured into the empty pitcher, showing that we draw from the community, but also give back. Individuals were invited to say to the total group what the community had meant to them or why this particular experience was meaningful. The entire congregation was also invited to make responses to those that spoke, which facilitated much personal sharing and responding.

Larry, my sons and I were the last to share. Neither son, in typical early teen fashion, had a great deal to say, but Larry had written a poem expressing his reaction to his previous experience with the group. When he began reading, he broke down, and it took him a few minutes to recover. I was so thrown by his response that my long-incubated, well-rehearsed farewell speech left me. I still have no idea what I said that day.

I began to wrap up involvements and projects in preparation for the move, one of which was my relationship with the United Methodist Church. As an ordained minister, I was currently appointed to St. Paul's, with the house church as an adjunct responsibility. In June, the Annual Conference of the Rocky Mountain Conference of the United Methodist Church would meet and the ministerial appointments for the following year would be announced. I had requested an educational appointment, having arranged to attend school at Emporia State University. To support myself, I had obtained a job directing a family resource center at the university, but that plan would not to come to fruition.

Three weeks before I was to arrive, *The Emporia Gazette* published a story with the headline "Gay Minister Enrolls in University", so before I ever arrived on the scene, my job and my anonymity disappeared.

> The car starts up…and yer heart takes flight.
> Then they knock you down…and they drive plumb outta
> sight!
> And then limping hop hop hop
> limping step step step
> limping drag drag drag
> Faaaallllll. (Hank collapses)

From *The Trials and Tribulations of Hank Cohen* by Julian Rush

When Larry called me about the article, I was shattered. I had worked hard putting everything together, ensuring that I was not leaving one job without having another. Now I had lost the position in Kansas, and all the fears about being unemployed, without money, and being badgered by creditors started closing in again.

By far, the most terrifying aspect of my coming out process had been the loss of job security. Never had anything happened to me in my entire life more unsettling than losing my position at First Methodist in Boulder. I was on my own and alone in a way I had never known before. Much earlier, I had moved out of the home shared with my wife and children, and before the divorce became final, I was carrying the house payment, loan payments, and paying my own rent.

After being released from the church in Boulder, my debts became so large that I lost all my credit cards. I was unable to continue making church pension fund payments for myself, and, for the first time in my life, began buying my clothes at garage sales.

While job-hunting, I went through fifty-one face-to-face contacts. Only when I secured the Chrysalis Project position did I began receiving a salary again, along with additional income from the house church.

When I had pursued career counseling earlier, I had interviewed people in businesses to find out what they did and how they got their jobs. I focused on public relations, since that seemed to be the area most closely related to my experience and skills. The process produced one clear realization for me: the business world didn't view ministers as having any marketable skills at all.

I had never had to sell myself for a job in my whole life, but on the open market, I understood I would be starting at ground zero. My age was a deterrent as well. Some companies might be willing to invest in a young employee for retraining, but few would be interested in retraining someone forty-five years of age. When I was hired as a temporary employee at Resource Electronics to market circuit boards, I was relieved.

My first week on the job, I was still a janitor at Wesley Foundation, and the Chrysalis position was not yet on the horizon. I was an anonymous person sent over from the temp agency to sit in a back room and do a three-week sales promotion. As ignorant as I was of circuit boards, at least I was away from the church uproar, newspaper commentary and public eyes, and I was making a little money. You can imagine my burst of panic when, in my second week, a woman walked up to me in the office and said, "Oh, you're Julian Rush, aren't you?" My reaction must have been evident, for she quickly revealed she was Velma Davis and had met me years before at a church gathering. She had followed my pilgrimage in the papers and couldn't believe I was forced into the position in which I now found myself. We went to lunch together, where she told me that she and her former husband had been working in gay rights for years. While meeting Velma at Resource Electronics turned out to be positive, the panic of that moment of discovery had stayed with me, and now resurfaced with *The Emporia Gazette* disclosure. The reporters had found me again, causing me to lose my job in Emporia before I had even arrived to claim it.

It was too late to back out on moving to Kansas, but I came close to doing just that. I thought, "I can't do this. I have no guarantee that anything is going to work. Here I go, headed off to Kansas with no job and no real assurance that the short-term relationship Larry and I share will last."

During my last two weeks in Denver, I visited various friends and acquaintances. Even though I didn't say the words, I was hoping somebody would talk me out of going. I knew there were people who felt I was making a mistake, that to pull up roots and move to Kansas was ridiculous. ("You're moving to **WHERE?**") Despite the lack of support from some, and in the face of all the odds, I still decided to leave. Deep inside I sensed that what Larry and I shared was real and worth going for.

I planned all along that my sons would go with me and spend their summer vacation in Kansas before returning to Colorado. When the time came to pack, they were part of the process. I looked through everything, held out only what was absolutely essential, and they looked through all the rest to see if they needed or wanted anything before we disposed of it.

I had kept my notes from seminary classes, occasionally referring to them for sermons and other projects. Assuming now that my church life would be limited, I threw them all away. Upon reflection, I realized that the notes were nearly twenty years old and out-of-date, but at the time it seemed like a drastic move.

I owned two cars: an old Karmen Ghia with 140,000 miles, and a Ford station wagon recording 110,000 miles. I had kept both because at least one was working when I needed a car. Now, with an imminent move, I sold the Karmen Ghia, and loaded everything into the Ford. There was room for the three of us to sit in the front seats, but the rest of the car was packed solidly.

The day before we left, I attended the Executive Session of the Rocky Mountain United Methodist Annual Conference, comprised of all the ministers gathered in yearly session. While there were still a few dissenting votes on my relationship to the connectional system, I was able to maintain good standing. My official position was secure and I could take my leave of Colorado.

The next morning the boys and I arose early and drove to Boulder for a farewell brunch with some house church folk. One young man in the gathering, a first year university student, took me aside and confided that I had given him the courage to deal with his own recognition that he was gay. While he had only revealed his sexual orientation to a few friends, he had finally taken the major hurdle of facing himself. He thanked me for helping him to see the possibility of living authentically as a gay Christian.

By midmorning, we were on our way to the Land of Oz. I had made arrangements for the three of us to spend the night in our sleeping bags at the Methodist Church in Burlington, Colorado, and the next day we completed our journey across Kansas. The closer Emporia became, the heavier my foot. We were expected to arrive late afternoon, but by three o'clock we were on Larry's doorstep. One of his brothers was visiting at the time we arrived, and seemed somewhat bewildered by the onslaught of kids, boxes, furniture and clothes.

The next couple of weeks were hectic, but there was an unaccustomed tranquility as well. The pressures of multiple jobs, goodbye visits and parties, church turmoil and interminable publicity had suddenly halted. By comparison, moving to Kansas and settling into a new town, home and friends was peaceful, even without a job. Everyone was warm and cordial, and I was welcomed with open arms.

The tranquility didn't last. Larry was willing to temporarily handle expenses, but I felt lost and directionless without work. I started visiting the Emporia Job Service (state employment office) twice every day, and checked the job service at the university regularly. I followed up on every possible lead, some as far as fifty miles away. About half held out some promise, but nothing developed until I interviewed for a minimum wage sales clerk position at Montgomery Ward. I took the job.

Learning the ins and outs of hardware, paint, plumbing, lighting and sporting goods was no little matter, and mastering the cash register was as trying for the instructor as for me. As depressing as the pay and work were for me, these were offset by being a functional part of society again, and engaged in a type of work I had never done in my entire life. Things seemed to be looking up. The boys were there, it was summertime and lots of activities were happening. I sought to keep my younger son occupied in a variety of ways, while my older son worked at odd jobs. Only after the boys left, when summer was winding down and the Wards job was becoming commonplace, did reality begin to set in. Larry and I began the process of learning to live together.

Both of us were the type of persons who, rather than making mountains out of molehills, made molehills out of mountains. We didn't like conflict, and apparently both of us had been doing a great deal of grinning and bearing the situation. In late summer, Larry and I began to deal with the realities. Larry, an individual who had lived alone for the majority of his adult life, needed his quiet time and private space. During the last few weeks not only did he have to adjust to another person living in the house, but two child-people underfoot also.

One blessing during this time was that it was summer, and he could retreat to the yard. Another was that he liked to rise early on workdays and spend thirty or forty minutes sipping coffee and waking up, when the boys were usually asleep. On the other hand, I am a fast morning starter, and, thinking this to be the perfect time for coffee and talk, soon learned that the last thing Larry wanted the first hour of the morning was conversation.

In addition to Wards, I was working on a church-related project begun early in the days of the house church. A minister I knew showed me how to organize a mail subscription service for the distribution of original hymns and liturgy. Since writing hymns and liturgies comes quite easily to me, I hoped I might build this service into a business by providing such materials quarterly. Gary Arnold, a minister with experience in public relations, and Ed Sanvold, my friend and co-worker at First Methodist, Boulder, helped me put together the package that we titled *Phoenix*. Included in each packet were liturgies for every Sunday in both traditional and contemporary styles, plus original hymns and other litanies for special occasions which might occur during that quarter.

From a mailing list of churches from several denominations, house church members helped me send out a partial *Phoenix* mailing which brought an encouraging amount of orders and cash for the first quarter. Some of the proceeds from the first subscriptions went to underwrite the second mailing, seeking more subscriptions. For the first and second mailing, I had begun with the areas of the country and the churches that I judged more likely to order the service. As a result, with each successive mailing the response decreased. Since I was using the money from each quarterly *Phoenix* subscription package to finance the next one, by the time number four was reached, there were no funds to continue. When the demise came, I didn't even have enough money for postage to explain to my mailing list. If someone wrote to inquire, however, I replied.

When I realized *Phoenix* was going under, the fears from months of uncertain employment surfaced once more. Each time I saw the possibility of crawling out of the hole, something would knock me back in again. This was not just the failure of the subscription service; this was a failure of my financial management. Once more I became aware of how insecure

I felt in the area of money. I had felt a letdown coming on well before the collapse of *Phoenix*, but now I slipped into a period of depression and discouragement. Of all the difficult times I'd suffered, this was the worst.

Philosopher:
Why can't we see tomorrow?
Could there be a crack in the crystal ball?
The future should look warm and sunny and bright,
But there is no promise of light.

Why can't we see tomorrow?
Could there be a flaw in the plan after all?
We wished for every dream to turn out just right,
But nothing is there but the night.

No vision here. Diagnosis unclear.
Breeding new fear and bringing sorrow, since
We cannot find tomorrow

There must be a crack in the crystal ball.
We keep awaiting dawn to come into sight,
But nothing is there…just the night.

From *The Rise And Fall of The Girl* by Julian Rush

The demise of *Phoenix* was not the only factor contributing to my depression. Finding a job other than the one I had at Wards seemed impossible. The only possibility that might have utilized my skills was a position counseling students with grade problems. I applied for the job, for which I was well qualified, but one week later the Kansas regents drastically cut funding at Emporia State, and the position went away with the funding. I became increasingly depressed about the job I held at Wards. I could do the work, but the tasks were mundane and without challenge. More than that, the pay was so low my financial crisis worsened. Even working fulltime, there was not enough income to meet expenses.

There was also the question of human service. I was unable to connect with a place where I could minister or use my time in a creative way. In Colorado, there had been the house church and St. Paul's, plus the drama surrounding the United Methodist Church homosexuality controversy, the activities of the Gay and Lesbian Community Center, and my work with Chrysalis. At this moment, Colorado looked like a rainforest and Kansas a desert.

There was also the loss of individuals who had made up my support group—friends who were hundreds of miles away, the fifty to seventy people regularly involved in the house church, the congregation of St. Paul's and my co-workers in other jobs. I was separated from a large group of people in Denver who, unlike residents of Emporia, valued and supported me, and knew who I was.

Larry and I shared his friendship group, which soon became mine as well, and I worked at Wards. That was it. Adding to the depression was the distance between my sons and myself. I couldn't be present for them in the way I wanted, and the way that I knew they needed. The contact which I maintained with them was not nearly as satisfying as physically being in their vicinity and available.

The loneliness was intense, and I responded by continuing to fix up the house. I built a trundle bed and bookcases in the boys' room so when they arrived again at Christmas they wouldn't have to sleep on the floor in sleeping bags. I repainted the living-dining area, moved furniture around, and added items here and there.

But a warm house doesn't make up for the loss of one's profession. After my arrival in Kansas, I contacted the United Methodist District Superintendent in charge of the Emporia area. While he was kind, he explained that I was now in conservative territory, and that the United Methodist ministers there were fearful of my visibility. He was correct.

When I visited the senior minister of First United Methodist Church, his response was predictably reserved. In addition, a nationally known church life expert, Lyle Schaller, had done a study with that particular congregation some months before, precipitated by the current pastor's inheritance of a difficult situation. Over time, the church had stabilized, but he felt that neither he nor the church could survive the kind of controversy that my presence might create. These experiences led me to make a conscious decision not to be involved in church activities at all.

The first Sunday after that decision, time was heavy on my hands. I had always spent most Sunday mornings in church. What could I do now? I began to develop a routine; instead of a cleansing of the soul I would achieve a cleansing of the clothes. On Sunday mornings I would take the dirty laundry and a make a pilgrimage to the laundromat. When I returned, Larry and I would put the clothes away and go to a nearby restaurant for brunch. After three or four months I began to realize that for a long time, I had been fulfilling my own spiritual needs in ways not directly related to the Sunday morning worship service. I had always been in a leadership position in worship, which meant concentrating on the doing and the coordination of the experience. I had been busy helping to create an experience for others, and had gradually begun to fulfill my own spiritual needs in other ways. The times I chose for meditation were occasions for spiritual renewal, for processing my feelings about the loss of church in my life, and the months of church-related events that had ultimately caused that loss.

I recalled the increasing difficulty of creating sermons for the house church in Boulder. In Kansas, I came to appreciate the stress that reduced my ability to function: the experiences I simply had not had time to process. In the slower lifestyle of the Kansas plains, I was able to find time to make contact with my hurt and anger and resentment.

Kansas was quiet, but it was no cocoon. My protection cracked open and there was only a half-finished butterfly inside. I was forced to face all the disgusting, ugly, cruel and malicious aspects of the situation which brought me to where I was. My exile was not only valuable, but essential. I needed to be totally separated from the institution of my discontent in order to do the processing required for growth. The hostility I felt about the church, and my place in it, needed to be exorcised. My support group was no longer present to insulate me. This was my own journey now.

During this low time, I slept a lot. When I was awake, I didn't function very well. My feelings were on my sleeve, and at the slightest comment tears would spring to my eyes. I attacked the pain with food, gaining about fifteen pounds.

I was trying to live out what I had learned from Anne Schaef: when you are depressed, *do* the depression. Don't ignore the feelings and the reactions and the stress. Face the reality of the depths of despair and the causes of the pain will open opportunities for options. The act of really *being* depressed was an effort. I found it hard to make honest contact with my feelings. One reaction was to cry. After Larry left for work, I tried to make contact with my sadness and hopelessness and release the feelings from deep inside myself. They came out in tears, and over time I found that the tears cleansed and restored me.

After three months of misery, the depression began to lift. The internal processing had undoubtedly helped, but there were three other significant changes which offered hope and new options: (1) After ten months of minimum wage in hardware sales at Wards, I was moved into a commission position in automotive, selling tires, which doubled my salary and removed some of the severity of my financial situation. This change imparted a self-confidence that I would be able to survive. Later, when I picked up a part-time house-painting job, I began to feel for the first time that even if the doors of the church never opened again, there would always be some way that I could make a living; (2) Larry and I began to talk about moving back to Denver, which would give me more career possibilities than Emporia could offer; and (3) I was one of a half-dozen people who engineered the formation of a lesbian/gay group on the Emporia State campus. Thirty people attended the first meeting, where we drew up a proposal requesting that the group be recognized as a legitimate campus activity. That way, resources such as advertising in the campus paper could be made available. A few objections were expressed when the proposal was presented, but the group was officially recognized. We then expanded our focus to include people in the community who were not students, and the group became a source of nurture for us all.

The religious groups on campus sponsored a workshop entitled "Loving" which attracted about three hundred people. Presenters included a nun, a divorcee, a young unmarried woman who was living with a man, a Church of Christ minister and myself as a gay minister. The Church of Christ is not known for liberal positions, and this pastor was absolutely predictable. During the workshop he said to me, "Julian, I feel even sadder about you after meeting you face to face. You're such a nice-looking person to be wasting your life in sin. I'm sure you're sincere about what you're doing, but frankly, I would rather have my son dead than have him be gay!"

> *Both:*
> He has to be stopped.
> He's obsessed with this lunacy,
> Blinded by zealots who foster the "way."
> He has to be stopped.
> He is bound for destruction now
> Unless we can conquer those dreams of decay.
>
> *Simeon:*
> He has to be stopped,
> And regardless of outcome, whatever discomfort or strife.
>
> *Sarah:*
> He has to be stopped
> For whatever the outcome.

Simeon:
His change.

Sarah:
His repentance.

Both:
His life!

From *P.T. Was Here* by Julian Rush

Ray, a longtime friend of Larry's and a teacher at Emporia State University, had become a friend of mine also. There were two administrators on campus who had discriminated against Ray because he was gay. Ray had taken the case to court, but the opposition had mired the works so successfully that the proceedings dragged on for five years. Ray became so disillusioned that he sought other legal advice, but when the first attorney discovered what was happening, he immediately dropped Ray's case and put a lien on it to prevent any other attorney from taking over. Several days later, our friend Ray was found dead in one of the university parking lots. The pressure was too much to endure, and Ray had killed himself. He left a letter in which he requested no funeral service. As a consequence, much pain about his death remains unresolved. Ironically, his former minister was the same man who had denounced me in the public meeting.

He has to be stopped.
For whatever the outcome.
His change.
His repentance.
His life.

Chapter Seven

I alternate between pain and rage when I see people suffer indignity at the hands of others. In the kinship of the struggle for dignity in this culture, I believe that all oppressed peoples are one. The cultural support for malevolent behavior is so pervasive that oppressed peoples are often not even aware of how their thinking and behavior oppresses others. I attended a Parents and Friends of Lesbians and Gays meeting in which the work of some creative lesbian and gay people was highlighted. Someone had the bad judgment to select the music of Stephen Foster and the entire group was asked to join in singing "Old Folks at Home" with the refrain "Oh darkies, how my heart grows weary." In an effort to celebrate the accomplishments of one oppressed people, this group was using words which supported the oppression of another. As the singing began, I remember flushing red and staring at the table in front of me. I was mortified that this was happening. I wasn't indignant or angry—I was hurt. My own support group was singing a song that oppressed blacks.

When I am in a counseling situation, I always try to remind people of how very fragile the human spirit can be. In the first weeks of my time in Kansas, early one morning I was sitting on the back porch in the sun drinking coffee with Larry. I don't recall what we were talking about, but I said something that Larry felt was abrasive. I will never forget the look of hurt on his face. Since then, I have become increasingly aware that making feelings known continues to be important, but how those feelings are expressed is even more critical.

In the process of our time together, Larry and I both made significant changes. For me, the energy spent on learning better ways to live in the relationship was partly an effort to reduce the chance of making the same mistakes twice. After fourteen years of marriage, then the separation and divorce, I resolved that if I ever again became connected to another person, I would try very hard to make it work.

I've always felt if two people really care about one another, the relationship will allow each to incorporate the other's spaces, instead of simply growing apart. In my attempt to incorporate Larry's spaces, I decided I needed to learn to play bridge. This would enable us to go to friends' houses together and play bridge as partners. I have always disliked card games, particularly those which require me to remember specific cards, who has them and who played what. My response has always been "Who cares?" And I don't like having to remember numbers. Yet, steeped in good intentions, I set out determined to become a good bridge player. After Larry saw me turn into a disagreeable old troll three or four times, he gave up on teaching me. I was not heartbroken.

> One thing you must admit before you run.
> We two would make a better pair than one!
> We've surely had some difference of opinion now and then
> For we approach our work in such distinctive ways.
> But strong willed people such as we know just where to begin,
> When they've discovered that some compromising pays.
> If we can keep our songs in tune, then I surmise
> That we can
> Harmonize!

Some couples may enjoy the same exacting melodies,

While others skip through life in perfect three-four
time.
I'm sure there may be some who, like the shining
Pleiades,
Create a symphony together that's sublime.
What if the two of us have our own tunes? You see,
We've still got
Harmony!

From *Jesusong* by Julian Rush

The most delightful aspect of possibly moving back to Denver would
be seeing my sons more often. The stay in Kansas had taught me the cost
of distance. When my sons left after the six-weeks summer visit, I hadn't
anticipated the length of emotional time between summer and their next
visit at Christmas. I called them at least twice a week, sometimes three
times, but the calls couldn't match personal contact. In order to lessen the
separation, I sent them letters every week, not just with news about myself
but with all kinds of activities for them—fill in the blank, solve the riddle,
and figure out the puzzle. A rude awakening came when I discovered they
were so involved in their own activities that weeks on end would go by
before they would fill out the sheets. Even when they did, they would mis-
place them or forget to mail them.

The separation grew more difficult, so as the holidays approached, I put
a great deal of time and energy into planning for the Christmas visit. The
boys' room looked fresh and tasteful with a new bedspread and matching
valance at the window. I bought Christmas presents, planned events and
meals for us to share. On Christmas morning, when they were to arrive,
Larry and I drove seventy miles to the Wichita airport only to discover the
plane from Denver would not be coming. That was the year of the huge
Christmas blizzard in Denver, and all planes had been grounded. When we
got back home, we found they had been trying to call.

The next day the boys boarded a bus in Denver for a fifteen-hour journey to Emporia. By the time they arrived, they were totally exhausted, and could have cared less about Christmas presents, food or anything else. They slept most of the next day. I was very disappointed; three days of the much-hoped-for time with my sons had been summarily wiped out by the storm.

I talked with a gay man recently who mentioned he had not seen his three children in several years, by choice. I couldn't comprehend what that would be like, or why someone would want to do that. The boys are all-important to me. I delight in the excitement and joy of being part of their lives as they emerge as human beings in their own right. They are important to me as people, not just as my offspring, and I have tremendous investment in them as global citizens of the future. Part of my investment is the deep desire not to let them down. On a daily basis I wrestle with my behavior with them at any given moment, over against the hopes and dreams of a future for them. I know that some of what has happened has been very disruptive to their lives, and they are bound to have feelings of resentment about dear old dad putting them through all this.

There are people who have criticized me severely for being selfish, self-centered and publicity hungry, accusing me of ignoring the impact of my life on my two sons. I had always insisted on having a primary role in nurturing them, and it was very difficult for me to separate that nurturing care for my children from my own attempt to be as authentic a person as possible. In my better moments, I'm convinced that the greatest gift I can give my sons is my authenticity. I can't do my years with them all over again; but if I could, I don't believe I could do it any other way. Going through the struggle I have experienced has gifted me with an openness and a freedom to love and accept and affirm other people that was never there before.

> Should there be any chance to try it all again, I would decline.
> We did it well. To change would be a masquerade.
> The scene's been played.
> From *The Man Who Can Save the Day* by Julian Rush

Having said all that, sometimes I still hurt.

There was a period when my anger was paramount. Time, perspective, and the love of many people have exorcised that anger, but the hurt remains. I hurt because my mother hurts for me; because the person with whom I spent fourteen years in a marriage relationship feels betrayed and used; because the "misty water colored memories of the way we were" are obscured by the way we are; because the joy of my struggle (that unbounded joy of at last being able to be who I am) cannot be shared with everyone I care about; because my two children had to be hurt and continue to be hurt in the process; because I cannot make everything easy for them; because they are not old enough to understand fully the painful mandate of my coming out process; because my partner hurt for me and for my children; because I could not make it easier for him; because there are old friends who have closed their doors to me; because there are old friends who insist that nothing has changed, but cannot bring themselves to tell me that nothing will ever be the same again; because there are old friends who accept me even though they cannot understand, and I know I cannot "make" them understand; because there are people who will not look me in the eye; because there are people who regard me as sick or despicable, and I hurt because there are people who resent my presence in the church. I hurt, but I hope that the pain never leaves, because in the agony of the process, I continue to realize a new depth of compassion and urgency about life which was never mine before.

Mantis:
When you fall in the forest and skin your knee,
It's a pain that's unpleasant to feel.
But in no time at all you've forgotten your fall
And the sore place will rapidly heal.
But a sore on the inside is not the same
Since a hurt on the inside hurts more.
'Tho' the pain that you feel will eventually heal,
It needs loving and caring and more.

A hurt on the inside is hard to erase,
So you need lots of time and a most quiet place.
A place you can shed your facade.
Just you and the quiet and God.

From *The Resurrection Thing* by Julian Rush

My time in Kansas was drawing to a close. One of the surest signs of my needing to leave was my inability to write. I had assumed that if I were living in any location that afforded me a quiet place, then I could write—plays, music, liturgy, whatever. With no distractions, my output would be voluminous. During the year prior to moving to Kansas, I kept yearning for more time to write. Suddenly, in the quiet of Kansas, there was no outlet for the human service part of me, and the flow stopped. I hadn't realized that the streams of words and music which had poured from my pen were the result of God's rainfall on the jagged mountains of human experience—the ups and downs, thrills and fears of people whose lives I had touched in ministry. With that crucial segment of myself on hold, the rain ceased.

I do not accept the theological stance that when good things happen, God has blessed us "real good", but when bad things happen, somehow we're being punished. I do find that there are times in our lives when events seem to converge in a way that makes sense emotionally and practically and spiritually. What's happening to us, or with us, or in us, seems "in sync"—just the right thing at the right time.

Larry and I had decided that, because the boys needed me and I needed them, we would relocate in Denver. To make that happen, Larry was willing to leave his home and give up a good position he had held for six years. Between us we had contracted that one of us would have to secure a substantial job before we would make a move. Larry sent applications to educational institutions and I applied for a transfer to a Wards store. Finally the waters parted. Within a three-day period I received notice of my

Wards transfer, plus an offer to become the director (part-time) of the Colorado AIDS Project. The time was right.

Group:
Things are gettin' better, better all the time.
Things are gettin' better, better all the time.

Jeannette:
We've had such a wait now, almost anything would look great now!

Group:
Better, better all the time.

Mr. Johnson:
Noah had to steer through a flood before he ever saw a rainbow in the sky.
Daniel had to brave it in the lions' den until he realized he wouldn't die.
Even brother Job had a long delay for an answer he could justify.

Jeff:
Jonah thought the fish had made a meal of him until deliverance at last arrived.
Moses feared that he and all the Israelites would be undone, but then they all survived.
Jericho had walls that were oh, so tall, Joshua had to have his faith revived.
Things are gettin' better, better all the time.

From *Don't Take It So Hard, Mr. Johnson* by Julian Rush

I relocated to Denver October 1, 1983, and Larry and I moved all of our possessions the week before Thanksgiving.

Back in Colorado, one of my agenda items for the Rocky Mountain Conference of the United Methodist Church would be to make plans about my next appointment. The Bishop and Cabinet preferred placing me with a congregation as soon as possible, and by April 30, 1984, St. Paul's United Methodist Church voted to restore my unpaid status, with the hope of finding a part-time salary. At the June Conference I was officially appointed to St. Paul's, and by fall, a salary was created. This offered me the opportunity to leave Wards (*Deliverance!*), begin a part-time position at St. Paul's, and spend the rest of my time with the AIDS project.

When I went to the personnel director at Wards to inform her I was leaving, I felt a great weight lift from my shoulders. I had spent two and one-half years of my life at Wards, which seemed like forever. Wards had provided income security, but now I could turn to other sources. I was glad to be free.

I'll never forget sitting in the cafeteria at Wards one day, overhearing a retired employee talk about his career. He had joined Wards twenty years before in a temporary job because he couldn't find the work he wanted. He stayed on, longer and longer, because still nothing better came along. At some moment he suddenly realized he had been there twenty years. The story was unsettling to hear. I thought to myself, "Dear God, don't let this happen to me."

The most stressful aspect of the Wards job was the boredom, because there was never anything new or challenging. Not one single aspect of what I did at Wards fulfilled me. The income was on the low side of fair, but not enough to make the deadness of the job worthwhile. In addition, having been used to a steady income, the erratic payments of commission sales was difficult. All my previous work experience had been as a professional, with the ability to determine my own schedule. At Wards, I punched a time card and was told what to do by people half my age and training. Getting out of that environment gave me new life. I hadn't realized how little control a person had in an organization like Wards until I wrote a letter to the national president protesting a particular quota system. People around me were buzzing about the fact that I had written the letter. A process that I saw as obvious wasn't even something that occurred to them. Most of them felt very imprisoned by the system, and I'm sure the Wards organization was able to operate quite comfortably on that assumption.

If all the employees stood tall and became intentional, the organization would have to change. Many of the clerks I knew felt victimized. If they stepped out of line they feared they would lose their jobs. Nothing made this clearer than the manager of automotive trying to enforce a quota system in our store. He didn't like it, but was under mandate from his superior. He was not about to put his job in jeopardy to protect his employees. And so it goes up the ladder. Even if one was willing to protest but the superiors were not responsive, nothing had to change. Wards had a statement to be signed by potential employees stating that the organization, like the employee, could terminate without notice or reason.

The system was misleading. On one occasion, all the employees were thanked. Small group meetings were held in which we were told, "You have helped Wards make money. You are important to us." The token of appreciation was a key ring. This was blatant doubletalk, and I said so to the group. I was totally offended by the exercise because every day Wards was indirectly telling my fellow clerks, and me "You, as a person, are not important. You are dispensable. Do it our way or we'll find somebody who can."

The game itself was extremely simplistic, designed with no input from local employees. By contrast, in my church experience, we as pastor, laity and other staff created our agendas together and carried them out.

There are two theories about power that I like to contrast. One says that all the power you have is what is specifically defined for you to exercise. The other says that you have all the power except what you are specifically forbidden to do. In this theory, persons believe that they have the right to do anything except what the rules say they cannot do. I usually operated in this latter style; Wards operated in the former.

A church example of the latter form of power was the vote of approximately six hundred to four hundred of the national United Methodist Church in 1984 that "self-avowed, practicing" homosexuals could not be ordained or appointed. This meant that I, as an openly gay pastor, faced the possibility of not being appointed again to a church. Until the national delegates changed their collective mind, retaining me as a pastor of a United Methodist church would be questioned. However, the individual regional Conferences reserved the ultimate power of making such a decision. The Rocky Mountain United Methodist Church Conference chose the understanding of power that says, "unless we are restricted from this particular action, we have power to exercise responsibility," and I was able to maintain my appointment to St. Paul's.

There are many people in the Rocky Mountain Conference who say to me by their words and actions, "You are important to us. We want you to stay." Some of them feel strongly that the Rocky Mountain Conference is setting a positive example for national United Methodists. Others want me to stay within the Conference and be employed by a church because I am "Exhibit A." Continuing support of my ministry is a clear way to say, "Lesbian and gay people are important to us. With you, Julian, as a tangible focal point, the war is easier to wage. Effectiveness is increased when the opposition must contend with not only an idea, but a real live person."

The necessity of maintaining my status as Exhibit A is actually an act of presence: "being there" as a primary function. I sometimes resented the time, energy and emotional drain, but I recognized that the responsibility of my presence and commitment in this time and place was crucial. An offshoot of this resolution was that the publicity didn't impact me so negatively as before. Seeing myself in print became so commonplace that I didn't bother reading most of the articles anymore.

Initially, having the national United Methodist church say, "we don't want you any more" led me to want to say, "Forget it! You're not worth the energy. I can do ministry elsewhere." Even though I don't act on those feelings anymore, the rejection of homosexual people in ministry causes me to keep defining what worthiness in ministry means for all.

I was called by God into ministry, and into the particular context of the United Methodist Church. I'll always be Exhibit A to some, but the central reason I'm still here is because God called me to be, and by golly, we're still doing business!

Chapter Eight

Comments by the Director/Composer, Julian Rush:

[Appropriating the words of Finley Peter Dunne, some preachers are known to explain] the central core of the Jesus Christ event as two fold: to comfort the afflicted and to afflict the comfortable. If Jesus were engaged in an earthly ministry now…His presence and message would be just as abrasive and unsettling to us as they were to those establishment people in 33 A.D., and that we would be looking for another kind of man to save the day for us.

From the Program Notes of *The Man Who Can Save The Day*
by Julian Rush

Conveying my understanding of the Christian message through writing plays and music has been integral to my life. When I'm creating, I find exciting things happening. One year in Boulder I had been working on a particular song for a play, but nothing seemed to come together. Suddenly one night I woke up at 4:00 A.M., went to the piano and the song was all there. I couldn't write it down fast enough, and was so exhilarated that I couldn't go back to bed. The creative process is sometimes a bit frightening, because I experience something flowing out of me full born in a way I can't explain.

When I sit down and take the time to concentrate on a particular theme or idea, I am aware of opening myself up to the "out there" and listening. And waiting. There are times when I find the music and words flowing out on paper and I know it's something beyond myself; I have been able to create words, music, or both, which give people insight. The way the lyrics and music come together helps them to see or understand a particular thing in a way they never did before. When people recall a particular song or hymn I've composed, I look back now, smile to myself and think, "Gee, did I really come up with that?"

The most frustrating condition to evolve out my coming out process is my lack of creative outlet for the messages that well up inside me. When I'm unable to write, I'm held back from connecting with one of the sources that gives me central meaning and focus; I'm separated from my identity. When I left First United Methodist in Boulder, except for a few months with the house church, most of my creative outlets disappeared. As a part-time associate pastor at St. Paul's, there was opportunity for me to create, but again, AIDS work soaks up sixty to eighty hours a week. I don't have the energy or time to create words and music as I used to. To understand that the circumstances of my life prevent me from tapping into the flow which waits for my response is disturbing. Every week we find ourselves in a slightly different place in the way we see and understand life and as each week passes, I feel I may be missing the chance to give birth to something that might be unique and special.

I have an abundance of people and situations to feed my experience bank as the AIDS Project unfolds, but there is rarely a block of time where I can reflect on what is going on. My creativity requires a delicate balance between external stimuli and internal creative time. The extensive mental processing I had to undergo after the loss of my Boulder position consumed me for a while, and the financial stresses which I faced so abruptly also contributed to the drying up of my creative juices. Now with AIDS becoming an ever-growing threat, I see my job with the Colorado AIDS Project as a calling. I'm here at this particular place in time with this unique opportunity, and I can't turn it loose. It's too important. When I look around me and see so many people dying, and see where I am and what I'm doing, I know that despite a lack of writing and composing time,

I'm doing what I need to do and I'm in one of the places I need to be. The Catch-22 aspect is still there, since my commitments to the Project feed my creative urges at the same time they devour the time I require to be open to the creative process.

Through all my years of ministry prior to Boulder, I led a rather sheltered existence. I believed strongly that the Church was a primary change agent in society. Since Boulder, I've experienced firsthand the Church as a strong preserver of the status quo. There are always individuals who serve as change agents in congregations, and even whole congregations that do. At the same time, I've experienced an institutional structure that proclaims sisterhood, brotherhood and unconditional love, yet continues to discriminate in administrative decisions. I've seen a structure that preaches love, then sets up carefully guarded conditions for applying it, placing economics above human rights.

People may point to my work at St. Paul's and say, "See, the church isn't so bad after all. Here's an example of one who is still able to participate." I don't want people to be able to whitewash their bigotry with that kind of a rationalization. The same kind of behavior is expressed when people say to me, "I accept you as a gay person, but I can't bring myself to allow you to be in ministry." That's comparable to, "I like black people, but I just don't want my sister to marry one." Some have said to me, "I love you as an individual, but I cannot tolerate you as a minister." That doesn't work with me. God called me into ministry, and anyone who cannot accept me as a minister is a person who cannot accept *me*. If love is unconditional and if I'm worthy as a human being, then I'm worthy as a tire salesman, as a father, or even, God forbid, as a homosexual minister.

There was a time in my pilgrimage when I could say to people, "It's all right if you can't accept me. I'll be patient and we'll grow together." I don't have time for that anymore. It isn't all right for people to reject me or anyone else from a stance of bigotry. The world we live in today can't sustain such attitudes if the human race is to survive. Such closed-mindedness has to be challenged and changed! We've been patient too long.

Two of the local churches in which I've engaged in ministry were strongly concerned with saving themselves and perpetuating themselves as bastions of ministry for the future. I won't be silent about such entrenched thinking anymore. I am committed to concentrating my efforts to create and sustain groups and structures that are open to healthy change—where change is not only possible but actually takes place.

People are like concrete culverts or pipes, the kind that go under roads for drainage. Sometimes the pipes get blocked with sticks, rocks and mud, and the water can't flow through. For me, living in a full Christ-awareness means keeping myself totally open, allowing the winds and waters of life to blow and flow through. Part of the continuing human struggle is to rid ourselves of the sticks, the rocks and the mud, and to remain open. I believe that today's Church has that responsibility.

Now I can look back at those last few months at Boulder and wish that I had been more intentional about dealing with the church while the church was dealing with me. Unfortunately, I was so overwhelmed with events at the time, I was unable to be centered. I felt that I was not in control of my destiny. I have been told in very sincere and caring terms that if I would disappear as a "gay minister", just quietly step aside, someone else would take up the gauntlet. Personally, I wasn't acquainted with anyone who was standing in line to do that at the time. There were also persons telling me that I had to keep on fighting for everyone's rights. If I wanted to walk away, I was reminded that such an action would affect not only my life, but also those in the larger United Methodist church body who were fighting for change.

I'd been pushed around enough, inconvenienced enough, frustrated enough, enraged enough, and bruised enough to be at that delicate point where I could have walked away and not looked back...but I didn't, and I'm glad I didn't.

Thomas:
I'm tired of everything and

Everyone who's pushing me, so,
Keep your place…and give me space…and

Don't step on my sandals.
Give me room to roam around.
I dislike being crowded and I refuse to be pushed,
Although my self-control's astounding when it's put to
the test.
So weigh all of your judgments
Before you utter a sound,
And don't step on my sandals,
Give me room to roam around.

From *Jesussong* by Julian Rush

How could it possibly be I was chosen?
What have I got?
What did I do?
Why should it have to be me that was chosen?
Why won't some other guy do?
I've been the most loyal Pharisee ever,
Faithfully trying to walk in the "way."
Why should I find myself forced now to sever
Ties that I cherished some easier day?
How could it possibly be I was chosen?
What have I got?
What did I do?
Why should it have to be me that was chosen?
Why won't some other guy do?

From *P.T. Was Here* by Julian Rush

Had the worst-case scenario developed and, via church court proceedings, I had been forced to relinquish my credentials, it wouldn't have been the end of the world for me, though I might have thought so at the time. Life would have gone on. In the last few years I've experienced the spirit winds blowing in a variety of places, and I know the institutional halls of the church are not God's last chance. I have learned I don't have to be within the institutional walls to do God's work. Since the events of Boulder, I have been deeply involved in two ministries markedly different from local church ministry, yet profoundly and spiritually demanding.

I obtained a position as street worker for Chrysalis shortly after leaving Boulder. The major part of my job description there was working with young prostitutes, male and female, ages eighteen through twenty-five. I was responsible for maintaining regular contact with each of them, doing individual counseling, and being out on the streets to make contact with our Chrysalis participants as well as those unfamiliar with our program in order to get them off the streets and, hopefully, out of prostitution.

Most of the young people I had worked with in church settings were from middle or upper class and stable family situations. In addition, they were comparatively sheltered and naive about the world outside of their insulated environments. The Chrysalis young people, on the other hand, were almost all exclusively from tumultuous family situations and extremely streetwise. Before I was hired, one of the concerns of the Chrysalis Director was that a person with my background might not be savvy enough to handle street folk, but I managed to adapt, stretch, and learn as I worked.

As a street worker, I obtained some of my success from the support of the young people who were already plugged into the program. They helped me contact other candidates for the program, and they went with me into the streets. At the time, making contact with male hustlers was easy because there was one designated area which was their turf. Females were harder to reach, since most of them worked with a pimp, who kept moving the girls around to elude the vice squad. When I wasn't on the streets, counseling, or handling administrative work, I spent time each week in the safe house for the young women as one of two supervising workers. We oversaw meal preparation and cleanup, study periods, miscellaneous activities, and generally acted as physically present adults.

Most of the Chrysalis youth lived at a level of intensity which I had not experienced with church youth. Sexual abuse was more the rule than the exception. Lives were case studies of crisis and trauma, and yet here these young adults were, trying to change their life patterns and deal with deep-seated issues of their not-so-distant past. The individual and group sessions were always tense and intense. Some examples follow:

➤ A young woman cried because she was part Japanese and part Black and felt rejected by both groups.

➤ A young woman remembered seeing her father walk through the gate when he deserted the family, and how for weeks she would sit watching the gate, expecting him to come back.

➤ A young woman with a black eye and a bruised arm said she would go back to her abusive boyfriend because he was the only person who loved her.

➤ A sixteen-year-old young man without parents told me he was gay, and that he was afraid to let anyone where he lived know, for fear of being abused by the older boys.

While I found the kids to be difficult, they were also hungry for affection and attention, and grateful for being recognized. Particularly, I recall one twenty-three-year-old Chrysalis young man who held on to me and cried when he discovered I was moving to Kansas.

The dramatic examples were no different in my work with the AIDS Project:

• A young man in counseling: "I'd like to go back to my church when I'm home visiting, but I've heard the minister say gay people are going to hell, so I don't feel comfortable being there."

- A female couple wanted me to bless their relationship in some way. Since the church wouldn't marry them, at least they could feel like they would experience a marriage of sorts.
- A young man related that when he told his divorced parents he was gay, the father was very understanding, but his mother never wanted to see him again.
- A person with AIDS confessed, "I can't believe this is happening to us."
- The man with AIDS asked me why his friends didn't come around any more.
- Another man with AIDS went to his brother's home for dinner, where everyone else was served on china plates with silverware while he was given a paper plate with plastic fork and spoon.
- A twenty-four-year-old stricken with AIDS walked away from me, looking like a stoop-shouldered man in his eighties.
- A heartbreaking situation: "My lover died two years ago. We had been together for twelve years. When he became seriously ill, his family came from California and wouldn't allow me in the hospital room to see him. When he died they took the body back to California, and I don't even know where he's buried."

For most people, living with AIDS is living on the edge of life. The more people I witness withering away one day at a time and dying, the more intolerant I become of intolerance about gayness or about AIDS. As the Colorado AIDS Project intensifies, I'm feeling more overwhelmed. Every week that passes, when I feel I can't handle more work volume or pressure, the volume increases and the pressure mounts, and like many others, I deal with it because the need is there.

A unique stress is rendered when one works with people who are dying and with people who are working with people who are dying. On one occasion I attended a memorial service for a man I had never met who had just died of AIDS. I had only known his lover previously. One of the friends read a statement written by the lover, thanking his deceased companion for all he had meant and been. It was genuinely moving. At the conclusion of the service, Neil, the surviving lover, announced that he had brought the Waterford crystal wine glasses and a bottle of wine that he and Rusty had used the night they committed themselves to each other. We were all asked to join in a toast to Rusty. As I was walking back to my car I realized I was crying and saying out loud, "It's not fair!"

Epilogue

Many years have passed since we first put my story into written words. Since then,

* My two sons grew up, went to college, and now both work overseas, living within the communities where they are involved.

* Larry was never happy in Colorado. We amiably decided to go our separate ways and Larry moved back Kansas to a small town where he still lives.

* The Rocky Mountain Conference of the United Methodist Church appointed me to the Colorado AIDS Project, where I continued to serve as Executive Director for seventeen years. I left the Project in March of 2001 for other pursuits.

* Churches across the nation began to designate themselves open to gay, lesbian, bisexual and transgendered persons by a classification recognized in their particular denomination. United Methodists selected the term "Reconciling Congregation" for those who considered themselves "open and affirming." First United Methodist Church of Boulder became a Reconciling Congregation in March 1997, and I moved my local church commitment back there in 1999.

"Let the circle be unbroken."

Fortuneteller:
When I see an old man withered by afflictions,
When I hear about a boy who never lived to be a man,
When I see a woman sitting all alone inside her bottle,
When I meet the girl who turned around and ran,
Then something deep inside me screams,
Though I know I can't control it,
Since the fates determine what events will be.
And I reach out to anyone who'll join their hands with mine
So that together we can face the mystery.

Philosopher:
When I hear the prophet shouting in his closet,
When I see the hungry children crying numbly in the rain,
When I watch the brilliant leader with his smooth unfurrowed forehead,
Or I meet someone who never felt a pain,
Then something makes me feel disgust
At the glimpse of such reluctance
To face life, and I deplore that such could be,
And I reach out [to] anyone who'll join their hands with mine
So that together we can face the mystery.

Priestess:
This world is full of people who hide behind a shell

Fortuneteller:
Because they're mad

Priestess:
Or wounded

Philosopher:
Or afraid of catching hell!

Priestess:
When I see the mouth that never hears my talking,
When I meet the friend who never knows my nature or
my name,
When I find a girl who never knew the baby or the father,
Or I'm stepped upon by those who play the game,
Then something deep inside me hurts,
And it hurts where I can't touch it
And I wish such pain would never, ever be;
Then I reach out to anyone who'll join their hands with
mine
So that together, we can face the mystery.

         *   *   *

The hurts still happen…I still get the arrows in my
       back like
Reject! Fag! Queer and such, but I can take the flack
Because I have a caring group who tell me constantly
That I belong. And what is more, I know that God loves me.
I can accept my difference now. If that's where I'm to be,
I thank you God for finding a place where I can be just
me.

A quiet place,
A loving place,
A special place.

From *The Rise and Fall of the Girl* and *The Man Who Can Save the Day*
by Julian Rush

About the Author

Rush and Ms. Merrick babysat each other's children in the '70s. Lee attended three plays produced by Julian and retained a warm friendship with him over the years. In 1984, both were Associate Pastors in St. Paul's UMC, Denver. Lee has published over 300 items, including the book *White Bird*.